Today's Ainu: Tales from Hokkaido

Kinko Ito, Ph.D.
University of Arkansas at Little Rock

For

Jason Peeler

With Much Love and Appreciation

Today's Ainu: Tales from Hokkaido

Contents

Preface

This is a book about the life stories of the contemporary Ainu people living in Hokkaido, Japan. It is an on-going, in-depth, ethnographic study of mine, which began in 2011. Chapter 1 introduces the readers to the basic information and statistics about the Ainu population, a few sociological concepts of race and ethnic groups, and the state of the people today. Chapters 2 to 5 cover the history and the world of the Ainu depicted in *GOLDEN KAMUY* (a very popular Japanese serialized *manga* and *anime*), my first encounter with the Ainu culture when I was a child living in Japan, and my first trip to the Ainu country in 2011. Some parts are my personal accounts regarding my family, the Ainu people, and their culture while other parts tell the readers how my ethnographical fieldwork began.

I asked my Ainu informants to tell me freely their experiences during my fieldwork in 2011, 2012, and 2014. Chapters 6 and 7 are about the life stories of two Ainu elderly men, who were my main informants. They let me stay in their homes for several days as if I were their family member. Their families and I did many activities together from sharing breakfast, helping with family chores, taking their dogs for a walk, going out to restaurants, visiting places that are historically significant to the Ainu, having afternoon tea, and nightly debates about the status of the Ainu. I was able to obtain a more detailed and intimate perspective of their daily lives. Chapters 8 and 9 briefly explain the Ainu language and religion, which will help the reader to understand what Mr. Nabesawa was talking about in Chapter 7 better. Chapters 10 to 13 are the stories told by two Ainu women in their 20s and early 40s, an elderly Ainu man who worked as an instructor of woodcarving, and a non-Ainu Japanese woman in her 60s who married an Ainu man. According to the official definition of the Ainu, this woman is "an Ainu."

The Japanese government declared that the Ainu are the indigenous people of Japan only in 2008. However, their ancestors lived in Hokkaido, the northern part of northeastern Honshu (mainland Japan), the southern part of Sakhalin, and the Kuril Islands since ancient times.[1] No native reservation for the Ainu has ever existed in Japan, and today, the Ainu's lifestyle is the same as any other resident's in the country. The majority of them live in Hokkaido and others reside in the greater Kanto area near Tokyo and Chiba.[2] The estimated number of the Ainu population fluctuates depending on the statistics and the researchers. Hokkaido Prefecture reported that there were about 17,000[3] Ainu in 2013, and the estimated number was about 13,318 in 2017.[4] Takuro Segawa states that there are 24,000 Ainu in Hokkaido today.[5] Regardless of statistical numbers, many government officials, scholars, and journalists assume that more Ainu people exist in Japan. They might not want to identify themselves as a member of the minority group, and many are not aware of their Ainu blood.

Many people think that Japan is a mono-ethnic country, but the minority groups such as the Ainu, resident Koreans and Chinese, *burakumin* (the untouchables), and Okinawans have been a part of the Japanese population for a long time. For example, the Ryukyu Islands are located between Japan, China, and Taiwan in the Pacific Ocean. The islands belonged to the

---

[1] Takuro Segawa. 2016, p.17.
[2] Yoshihiko Sekiguchi. 2007.
[3] Minako Sakata. 2018, p.5.
[44] Hokkaido Shimbunsha. 2018, p.33.
[5] Takuro Segawa, 2016, p.17.

Kingdom of Ryukyu and had their own culture. They became a sub-fief of the Satsuma Domain in the southern part of Japan in 1609. The Japanese government fully incorporated the kingdom into Japan in 1879, and today it is the prefecture of Okinawa.[6] The Ainu lived in Hokkaido and other locations that now belong to Russia, but they never had a nation of their own.

Figure 1 Soft drink vending machines painted with traditional Ainu embroidery motifs in white and blue.

The history of the Ainu is the history of an ethnic cleansing that officially began in earnest in 1869 when the Meiji Government renamed the Ainu's homeland Hokkaido and started colonization. The vigorous and forced assimilation processes on the Ainu began in 1871. The Ainu have experienced colonialism, settler colonialism, racism, exploitation, violence, oppression, and social stigma just like other indigenous people in North and South America, Oceania, and elsewhere.[7]

The Meiji government enacted the Family Registration Law in 1869. In Hokkaido, the completion of the Family Registration of the *Wajin* (non-Ainu ethnic majority Japanese) and the Ainu took place in 1873 and 1876, respectively. The Ainu became Japanese citizens whether they liked it or not.[8] On the other hand, those descendants of Korean or Chinese residents are not Japanese citizens even though Japan is the only country they know and they speak only Japanese. They go to Japanese schools, work, and act as any other Japanese, and many can pass as Japanese. However, when they go abroad, they need to obtain Korean or Chinese passports from their embassies in Japan. The visa requirements of certain nations also differ depending on which passport one has. My acquaintance once told me, "My husband was a second generation Korean resident whose parents came to Japan when Korea belonged to Japan. He was born in Japan, spoke Japanese, Korean, and English. He graduated from a university in Tokyo and worked for a trading company. He sometimes had problems getting visas easily when he went abroad to do business. He really wished he had a Japanese passport." The Japanese laws are supposed to protect the citizen's and residents' human rights and freedom, but persistent inequality still exists in Japan.

I began my ethnographic study of the Ainu people during my sabbatical during the spring semester in 2011. In fall 2010, the chair of the department asked me if I was interested in taking time off to do research. He asked me whether I wanted to keep researching Japanese *manga*

[6] Edwin O. Reischauer. 1990, p.127.
[7] ann-elise lewallen. 2016.
[8] Kato & Wakazono. 2018, pp.66-68.

(comics). I was finishing my manuscript titled *A Sociology of Japanese Ladies Comics: The Life, Love, and Sexual Fantasies of Adult Japanese Women* at that time and told him that I wanted to study something new. He said that I had two weeks to turn in the research proposal and application for my sabbatical. I thought I could easily come up with a new topic for my sabbatical in that timeframe. However, I received an e-mail from him the next day that the deadline was in two days instead of two weeks. I took out my binders of my sociology course on Japanese culture and society to look for a topic. I turned a few pages of my lecture notes and came to a section on the Ainu. My knowledge about this indigenous minority group at that time was just good enough to lecture to the undergraduate students for one class period. I also showed an educational video program on the Ainu, which was about 25 minutes.

My only Ainu connection had been a set of wooden bears carved by the Ainu artisans that my father brought me from his trip to Hokkaido when I was about 5 years old. The set consisted of a father bear, a mother bear, and their cub. My father used to tell me children's stories at my bedtime, and one of them was a story of a bear family. The Ainu men used to carve them and sell them as souvenirs in those days when tourism to Hokkaido was becoming very popular.

I love traveling. I have visited more than 80 countries and met various kinds of people from different racial and ethnic backgrounds including the indigenous people in the United States, Taiwan, Guatemala, Peru, Bolivia, and Venezuela. I usually go back to Japan several times a year to visit my family, but I had never met an Ainu person. An idea hit me for my sabbatical research proposal! *Why don't I go to Hokkaido, meet the Ainu, and study them?* I wrote my research proposal for my sabbatical in one day. My sweet childhood nostalgia added to the excitement of doing a new ethnographic study in Hokkaido.

The Dean of Arts Humanities and Social Sciences generously gave me summer scholarships in 2012 and 2014 so that I could continue my ethnographic research on the Ainu. I collected data by interviewing more than 30 Ainu and non-Ainu people during my field research. I also gathered my data by participant observation as I stayed in my Ainu informants' homes, attended lectures by the Ainu elders, and participated in their festivals.

My narratives in this book vary from one section to another. Parts of it read like a series of interviews in popular American magazines while other parts read more like a textbook. It sometimes might seem that I am bombarding my readers with Ainu and Japanese terminologies and words in certain parts, but I try to explain them as much as possible in the text or in the endnotes. In other parts, the Ainu people tell their story in a colloquial manner in their own words as they told me their stories. I kept and wrote their words and expressions. I recommend that my readers start with Chapter 1, but he or she can read the chapters in any order. Visual sociology utilizes visual information such as photographs, advertisements, and video clips for analysis. It provides a researcher with "new ways of conceptualizing and measuring aspects of our social world.[9]" I inserted more than 100 photos that pertain to Hokkaido, the Ainu people, and their culture, history, and traditions.

I appreciate all those people who participated in my interviews and offered me pleasant and nice homestays. So many people both in Japan and in the United States helped me throughout my fieldwork, and I am very thankful for the opportunities they provided me. My research endeavor has been like a journey, a long but very educational and emotional one.

---

[9] Curry and Clarke. 1978, p.1.

Chapter 1: Who Are the Ainu?

(1) The Ainu People

The original meaning of the word Ainu is "humans." It refers to (great) humans in general. The term is also an honorific for men, a name a wife calls her husband, or a name that refers to a child's father. The meaning of the word narrowed down to refer only to the Ainu themselves after their contact with the *Wajin* (non-Ainu ethnic majority Japanese) and Russians. A person must have certain characteristics in order to be an Ainu: brave, skillful, eloquent, and hardworking.[10] An Ainu who is lazy or who does not do his or her share of the work is not an Ainu but a *wenpe* ("a bad person").[11]

The ancestors of today's Ainu used to live in the *Ainu Mosir* (Ainu Homeland). The word literally means the earth where humans dwell, or peaceful, quiet land of humans. *Mosir* means island, territory, or nation. Their land was indeed vast and boundless covering the areas from the northern part of Honshu and Ezo (today's Hokkaido) to the Kuril Islands as well as the southern part of Sakhalin in the Sea of Okhotsk. *Ainu Mosir* also means "this world" as opposed to *Pokuna Mosir* (the world of the dead) and *Kamuy Mosir* (Gods' country).[12] Japan and Russia divided the land where the Ainu originally dwelled between them in the 19th century. The Ainu are not a monolithic group, and there are geographical and cultural diversities among different regions regarding their dialects, social problems, embroidery designs for ceremonial clothes, as well as customs, and manners.[13]

Today the Ainu people constitute a racial and an ethnic minority group of Japan. Dalton Conley, an American sociologist at Princeton University, defines race as "a group of people who share a set of characteristics – typically, but not always, physical ones – and are said to share a common bloodline."[14] The Ainu are also an ethnic group, which shares a distinctive cultural heritage and traits, including "common ancestry, language, or religion that gives them a distinctive social identity."[15] Fashion, food habits, national origin, and attitudes about certain things also characterize an ethnic group. We must note here that the concept of an ethnic group, like deviance, is socially constructed and their status is socially conferred. The prefecture of Hokkaido defines the Ainu as "those who appear to inherit the Ainu blood in a community and the people who share the same livelihood with them due to marriage or adoption."[16]

(2) The Ainu in Contemporary Japan

The Ainu of today reside mainly on the northern island of Hokkaido, which is roughly the size of South Carolina in the United States. Statistics published by the prefecture of Hokkaido in 2017 lists the number of Ainu households as 8,274 and its population as 23,782[17]. Cultural

---

[10] Ainu Minzoku Hakubutsukan. 2009, pp.12-13.
[11] Shigeru Kayano. 2004, p.5.
[12] Yoichi Tsunoda. 2018, p.14. Hideaki Uemura. 2008, p.13.
[13] Barbara Aoki Poisson, 2002. Ainu Minzoku Hakubutsukan, 2009.
[14] Dalton Conley. 2017, p.326.
[15] John Macionis. 2012, p.322.
[16] www.pref.hokkaido.lg.jp/ks/ass/H29_ainu_living_conditions_survey.pdf. P.1. Translation mine. Accessed 3/5/19.

Survival, an international organization, estimates that there are between 24,000 and 200,000 Ainu people living in Japan.[18] Thus, the actual number of the total Ainu population remains a mystery, and today full-blooded Ainu are very rare due to exogamy. According to the most recent statistics in 2017, there were 5,571 Ainu households in 63 cities, towns, and villages in Hokkaido and 13,118 people identified themselves as Ainu. In the previous survey in 2013, the number was 16,786.[19] There are about 5,000 Ainu people who live and work in Tokyo and its metropolitan areas.[20] These numbers are limited to only those who readily identify themselves as Ainu, and many say that the number could be significantly higher. Those who can pass as *Wajin* might want to hide their Ainu ancestry in fear of bullies and discrimination against them at school, at work, or in marriage.[21] The Japanese family registration paper does not require one to identify one's Ainu ancestry. Today, major Ainu communities are in Shiraoi (Shiraoi District), Nibutani (Biratori Town), Shizunai (Hidaka County), and Akan (Kushiro City) in Hokkaido.[22]

The Ainu live just like any other *Wajin* in contemporary Japan. The word *Wajin* used to mean those Japanese immigrants who came to Hokkaido before the Meiji Period (1868 – 1912), but today *Wajin* refers to the non-Ainu ethnic majority Japanese.[23] There are few, if any, communities where the Ainu are the majority in Hokkaido due to the governmental policies that affected them directly or indirectly.[24] At the same time, there are those Ainu people who would rather hide their roots, who are not interested in their traditions, or who want to remain aloof from anything Ainu. As stated before, they might want to avoid prejudice and discrimination. It could be just a part of the psychological stage in one's life. There are Ainu people who start to be interested in their roots in their middle age and pursue their ancestry by engaging in the traditional crafts work such as sewing, embroidering, and appliqueing. Others might start to take language lessons and practice their traditional oral literature.[25]

---

[17] www.pref.hokkaido.lg.jp/ks/ass/H29_ainu_living_conditions_survey.pdf. Accessed 3/5/19.

[18] Cultural Survival Quarterly. July 2001. www.culturalsurvival.org/publications/cultural-survival-quarterly/japans-ainu-seek-help-preserve-their-native-culture. Accessed 9/3/18.

[19] www.pref.hokkaido.lg.jp/ks/ass/H29_ainu_living_conditions_survey.pdf. Accessed 3/5/19. www.ainu-assn.or.jp. Accessed 8/29/18.

[20] Yoshihiko Sekiguchi, 2007. Minako Sakata. 2018, p.5.

[21] Hokkaido Shimbunsha, 2018. Shizue Ukaji, 2011.

[22] www.ainu-assn.or.jp. Accessed 8/29/18.

[23] FRPAC. 2010, p.4.

[24] Sakata, Minako. 2018, p.53.

[25] Hokkaido Shimbunsha, 2018. ann-elise lewallen, 2014.

Figure 2 The contemporary home of one of my Ainu host families (2014).

Figure 3 Mr. Kazunobu Kawanano, my Ainu host father driving me around town (2011).

Figure 4 Mr. Sohichi Kawanano is talking on his cell phone (2012).

(3) The Ainu as a Racial Group

The term race refers to "a group of people who share a set of characteristics – typically, but not always, physical ones – and are said to share a common bloodline[26]." According to an anthropologist Mary Inez Hilger, a full-blooded Ainu has fair skin, a long nose, round eyes, "curling lashes, prominent eyebrows, rather long earlobes, and an abundant head of hair, often with a slight wave" as well as body hair.[27] Full-blooded Ainu, according to Batchelor, are also "strong, thick-set, squarely-built and full-chested."[28]

Some of the Ainu women I met in Shiraoi and Sapporo indeed looked more Caucasian than Asian regarding their facial features. They had very fair skin, large eyes, and long nose. A young woman whom I befriended had beautiful eyebrows and lush eyelashes that many Japanese women envy. She showed me her arm saying, "This is what I do not like about being an Ainu. Look at my hairy arms!" In 2012, I also happened to see an Ainu man at a community parking lot where the people were listening to the campaign speeches for the mayor's election. He looked just like my Italian friend from Sardinia. I asked one of my Ainu informants, "Is he an Italian?" The answer was, "No, he is an Ainu." My informant, by the way, looked more like a Polynesian. The husband of one of my Ainu friends has eyes that are of green-hazel color. All the Japanese people I know have brown eyes of one shade or another, and I was quite surprised when I first met him. As for the skin color and facial features, the Ainu I met or saw pictures of in Hokkaido appeared to have descended from a diversity of regions; some resembled Italians and others Russians, Native Americans, Filipinos, and Micronesians. Dr. Hiroshi Ushiro, who is a curator of archaeology at Hokkaido Museum in Sapporo, explained to me that the ancestors of the Ainu could be a mixture of the proto-types of all the major races: Caucasian, Mongoloid, and Negroid.[29]

Takuro Segawa is an award-winning Japanese archaeologist and writer, who was born in Sapporo in 1958. He is now a professor at Sapporo University. He states in his most recent book: "I was born in Hokkaido, but I had not met an Ainu person before I went to Asahikawa. Some Ainu people were engaged in the excavation there, and I found their faces looking quite exotic. Among them were those who had the appearances of people from the Central and Western Asia as well as those who looked like a Roma, a European minority people. It was my impression that no wonder there have been numerous theories which argued that the Ainu belonged to the Caucasoid race."[30]

Europeans and North Americans first learned of the Ainu around the end of the 19th century. They were curious about the Ainu because they did not look like the ethnic majority Japanese. The early 1900s was a time when exogamy between the Ainu and the *Wajin* was not as popular as today. John Batchelor, a British missionary to Hokkaido who lived with the Ainu for many years, referred to the Ainu as "this strange race"[31] and "this ancient race."[32] Indeed, Ainu racial classification has been contentious. Some theories claimed that the Ainu were a proto-Caucasoid people who came to Japan through Siberia, while other theories tried to relate them to the aborigines of Australia.

Heinrich von Siebold (1852 – 1908) was a son of famous Philipp Franz Balthasar von Siebold (1796 – 1866). Siebold, the father, was a German aristocrat who worked as a resident

---

[26] Dalton Conley. 2017, p.326.
[27] Mary Inez Hilger. 1967, p.272.
[28] John Batchelor. 1892, p.18.
[29] Private conversation with Dr. Hiroshi Ushiro, 6/9/2012.
[30] Takuro Segawa. 2015, pp.18-19. (Translation mine)
[31] John Batchelor. 1892, p.8.
[32] Ibid. p.14.

physician and botanist in Dejima in Nagasaki. Japan had a self-imposed national isolation policy for many years during the Tokugawa Period (1603 – 1867), but a Dutch trading post was located in Dejima, a small artificial island. Philipp Franz Balthasar von Siebold introduced Western medicine to Japan, and he engaged in collecting ethnographic items and plants in Japan as well.

Heinrich, the second son of father Siebold, went to Japan with his brother after their father's death, and he worked as a diplomat and translator in the Austro-Hungarian Embassy in Edo (modern day Tokyo). He loved Japan and was interested in archaeology, ethnology, folklore, and Japanese culture. He said that the Ainu are the oldest ancestors of the Caucasoid. The World's Fair was held in St. Louis in the United States, the new gateway city to the undeveloped West, from April 30 to December 1 in 1904. Nine Ainu went to St. Louis, and several of them were on display in the Japanese pavilion, which included their traditional house *cise* (a thatched hut with a fireplace in the center). Other native people on display included the Apache of the American Southwest, Igorot of the Philippines, and the Southeast Alaskan Tlingit tribe. The Ainu people participated in the Summer Olympic Games of Aborigines held in August. Sankua Hiramura won second place in archery, and Rirotoke Hiramura won third place in the javelin throw.[33]

The theories of the Ainu's racial origin reflect the ideologies of the times. Europeans considered that the Ainu belonged to the Caucasoid race since the end of the 19th century. In 1937, Germany and Japan concluded a treaty that developed into the Tripartite Alliance with Italy in 1940. The Nazis controlled Germany at the time, which raises the question of why Germans wanted to conclude a treaty with an Asian nation when Nazi ideologies of racism were rampant. In fact, the Nazis considered the Ainu to be the original Japanese, a white race, and thus it was acceptable for the German people to be allied with the Japanese. Research has become more scientific and positivistic in modern Japan. Many technological developments took place in the methodologies of physical anthropology, computer science, and statistical analyses that have contributed to recent research findings.[34] The Japanese research flatly disproves the early surmises that the Ainu have Caucasian origins. In fact, the Ainu belong to Mongoloid, something that sequencing Ainu DNA has supported[35]. Recent research indicates that "the Jomon people bore considerable similarity to the present-day Ainu of Hokkaido" and that "the Ainu are unmistakably descended from Jomon people."[36] The Jomon people, the earliest inhabitants of Japan, engaged in primitive hunting, fishing, and gathering.

More recently, many investigations took place in the Hidaka Region in Hokkaido, and they revealed that the Ainu belong to Mongoloid. The discussion did not end there because the Ainu have many characteristics that are different from those of Mongoloid. Thus, some researchers including Segawa consider that the Ainu are "proto-Mongoloid" since they retain the characteristics found before the Caucasoid and Mongoloid races separated.[37]

We must not forget the existence of *Wajin* children adopted by the Ainu. Their parents immigrated to Hokkaido with high hopes of finding their fortune, but they went back to Honshu due to the hardship, especially during the winter. They left their children behind. There were also those parents who could not afford to raise any more children. Thus, the Ainu adopted and raised

---

[33] Hideaki Uemura. 2008, pp.58-61.
[34] Nobuyuki Ogasawara. 2004, pp.11-16.
[35] Nobuyuki Ogasawara. 2004, pp.11-16.
[36] Kenneth Henshall. 2004, p.11.
[37] Takuro Segawa. 2015, pp.19-20.

the newborn babies, some of who strongly identified themselves as Ainu even though they looked *Wajin.*[38]

Figure 5 Megumi Kawakami, an Ainu woman clad in traditional dress with elaborate embroidery and a headband. She is openly Ainu (2014).

(4) The Ainu as an Ethnic Group

Full-blooded Ainu people look different from typical *Wajin* people. Their number is actually very small today due to intermarriage between the Ainu and *Wajin* that took place after the Meiji Period (1868-1912) and over so many years. The Ainu actively promoted exogamy (out-group marriage) to reduce the amount of discrimination against their descendants. Hilger observed that "Now the Ainu, who stood apart for millenniums, face complete absorption by the Japanese[39]." She called the Ainu "a vanishing people." Are they really?

The Ainu are also an ethnic group with a subculture different from the mainstream Japanese culture (i.e., religion, language, food, traditional clothes, etc.) The Japanese government enacted the Ainu Culture Promotion Law in 2007 in order to preserve, disseminate, and promote knowledge about the Ainu traditions.[40] There has been much effort to maintain the popular dances, songs, arts, crafts, music, oral literature, cuisine, and other aspects of the Ainu life by the Ainu themselves, the *Wajin*, and the various cultural and educational organizations as well as research institutes. Many of them are very active in their efforts to preserve their traditions. In Hokkaido and elsewhere, certain universities, schools, and communities offer Ainu language classes. Ainu cultural centers and museums offer classes in Ainu design embroidery and teach how to make a *mukkuri* (a mouth harp). Ainu language speech contests, various rituals, and cultural festivals are held regularly year after year. Many names of places in Hokkaido originally derive from the Ainu language. In this regard, I consider that they are far from being "a vanishing people" as Hilger claimed.[41]

What about the indigenous American people? Have they vanished? We might not see many full-blooded people, but their legacies are still going strong here in Arkansas where I live

---

[38] Sohichi Kawanano. 2014. *Have You Heard about the Ainu? Part 2 Toward a Better Understanding and World Peace* (2015). YouTube.

[39] Mary Inez Hilger. 1967, p.268.

[40] www.ainu-assn.or.jp/ainupeople/overview.html. Accessed 2/15/2019.

[41] Mary Inez Hilger. 1967, p.268.

and teach. Many of the students in my classes, whether they are Caucasians, African Americans, Latinos, or Asians, have blood that is mixed with that of native inhabitants of the United States. Each of them looks very different, but they may share the same blood of an indigenous American among themselves. Arkansas also has many names of locations that derive from their languages such as Quapaw, Choctaw, and Ouachita, which many of out-of-state people find hard to pronounce. In Arkansas and neighboring Oklahoma, there are museums, preserved historic sites and houses, and research centers regarding the original inhabitants of the United States. They publish newsletters, books, and journals every year. The number of full-blooded Indigenous people might be decreasing but they still exist in people's mixed blood, location names, and history.

Figure 6 These people are clad in traditional clothing and are dancing at an Ainu Festival in Shizunai (2014). (Photo taken with permission of the group leader).

(5) Some Social Issues Surrounding Today's Ainu

The modern Ainu still tend to be negatively affected by the historical consequences of exploitation and oppression as much as the contemporary African Americans in the United States in general are still impacted by the legacy of slavery in regard to racism, economy, employment, morale, family, values, education, mentalities, food, and health.[42] Sakata states that Japan is a country where the Ainu people still feel rather uncomfortable to say they are Ainu while the number of people who claim that they are indigenous people is growing in the United States and Canada.[43]

The environment surrounding the Ainu has been going through a very rapid change politically and socially in recent years since the Japanese government's official recognition of the Ainu as the indigenous people of Japan in 2008.[44] However, the Ainu still tend to suffer from prejudice, discrimination, injustice, and poverty. Institutional racism has been systematically oppressing and exploiting the Ainu. Even though no Ainu families live in the traditional house

---

[42] Kayano, Shiro. In Kinko Ito. 2015. *Have You Heard about the Ainu? Elders of Japan's Indigenous People Speak.* YouTube. Hokkaido Shinbunsha, 2018.

[43] Sakata, Minako. 2018, pp.8-9.

[44] Kato & Wakazono. 2018, p.I.

due to the fire prevention laws, there is a significant gap between the living standards of the Ainu and the non-Ainu Japanese. For example, in 1986, the Japanese government reported that 2.19% of the Japanese depended on public assistance while 6.09% of the Ainu did. In 1999, the rate of Ainu on public assistance in Hokkaido was about five times as high as the national average, and in 2006, the rate remained about four times as high.[45] In 2006, the prefecture of Hokkaido did a survey on the state of the Ainu life and reported that the Ainu still suffer from a big gap in their standard of living, economic well-being, and higher education, as well as suffering discrimination. About 30% of the Ainu people reported having experienced discrimination by the administration, in obtaining employment, at work and school, as well as dating and marriage. These statistics do not include indirect and structural discriminations that arise from misunderstandings and ignorance.[46] The survey by the prefecture of Hokkaido in 2017 found that 36.1% of the Ainu people receive public assistance while the number for the rest of the people was 32.1 %. In 2013, the numbers were 44.8% for the Ainu and 33.1% for the rest. There is a significant decrease in number of the Ainu recipients. The rates of junior high school graduates going to senior high school were 95.1% for the Ainu and 98.8% for the non-Ainu students in Hokkaido. The rates of advancing to college or junior college were 33.3% for the Ainu while 45.8% was the prefectural average.[47]

As for education, in 1986, 94% of the Japanese attended senior high school, but only 78.4% of the Ainu did, even with scholarships from the Japanese government. Only 8.1% of Ainu attended universities, but the national average was 27.4%.[48] A 1993 survey in Hokkaido found nearly the same statistics: 87.4% of the Ainu went to senior high school and 11.8% attended universities, while the rates for non-Ainu Japanese were 96.3% and 27.5%, respectively.[49] A 2006 survey by Hokkaido prefecture found that 53.7% of Japanese studied at two-year junior colleges and four-year universities, 38.5% of non-Ainu Japanese in Hokkaido did, and only 17.4% of Ainu did.[50]

The Ainu experience discrimination at work, school, and in marriage. According to the statistics by the Hokkaido Utari Association[51] in 1994, 62% of the Ainu respondents said that they had not experienced discrimination in the last several years; 10.1% said that someone they know was exposed to the ill-treatment, and 7.3% of the respondents claimed that they were discriminated against. Discrimination took place when obtaining a job, at work and school, in dating and in refusals to marry, when dealing with the administration, and in verbal insult and negative comments on the respondents' looks and bodily features[52].

Many *Wajin*, unfortunately, are still ignorant of or indifferent to the Ainu, their history, and culture in the 21st century in spite of readily available social and mass media. Mrs. Sachiko Kibata, one of my Ainu informants, shared with me an interesting story during an interview in 2014. She has a *Wajin* daughter whom she adopted when she was a child. Mrs. Kibata said:

---

[45] Hideaki Uemura. 2008, pp.91.
[46] Hideaki Uemura. 2008, pp.90-93.
[47] www.pref.hokkaido.lg.jp/ks/ass/H29_ainu_living_conditions_survey.pdf. Accessed 3/5/19.
[48] Giichi Nomura *et. al.* 1996, p. 44.
[49] Nobuyuki Ogasawara. 2004, p.193.
[50] Hideaki Uemura. 2008, pp.90-93.
[51] Today's name of the Hokkaifo Utari Association is Hokkaido Ainu Kyōkai (Association). It was established in 1930, and it changed its name to Utari Association in 1961. The association changed it back to its original name in 2009. www.http://ja.wikipedia.org/wiki/北海道アイヌ協会.
[52] Nobuyuki Ogasawara. 2004, p.195.

"I once went to visit my daughter who lives in the central part of Japan. We went to a ramen noodle restaurant. The hostess and my daughter are kind of friends. She said 'The Ainu in Hokkaido are still living with bears, right?' I was totally shocked.

"My daughter said to the hostess, 'My mother is an Ainu.' The hostess did not believe it (since my adopted daughter does not look like an Ainu). She said, 'Your mother is too beautiful to be an Ainu.' Ainu women used to have tattoos around their mouths, and she still thought that all Ainu women have tattoos. Ainu men used to grow long beards, too. I told the hostess, 'I truly am an Ainu and teach the language as an instructor. I'm a real Ainu. Your view is anachronistic. Today the Ainu live in sturdy houses, and there are no beggars.' She was surprised to hear this and said, 'I'm very sorry. I need to learn more about the Ainu.' She also apologized to my daughter. People who know nothing about us still think the Ainu live in the wild. Her comments made me feel upset for a while, but I knew I shouldn't. I understood that it was because of her ignorance that she would say such things about us."[53]

In modern Japan, the Ainu still suffer from *existential inequality*, an inequality that "allocated freedom and unfreedom in the pursuit of personal life projects, rights and prohibitions to act, and distribute affirmations and denials of recognition and respect."[54] Many Ainu people who can pass as Japanese do not want to reveal their heritage due to stigmatization that produces existential inequality. Racism has been one of "the main, stark, classical forms of institutionalized existential inequality."[55] According to Therborn, "Ethnic existential inequality is still practiced in many places and ways, but it has become thoroughly discredited as a public explicit discourse."[56]

The Ainu have experienced the same kind of ill-treatment that every Indigenous group of the world have received in the United States. It was only on June 6 in 2008 that the Japanese government recognized the Ainu as an indigenous ethnic group and recommended that discrimination against them be terminated.[57] This should lead to the elimination of existential inequality and allow the Ainu people to expand their freedom to act and gain respect.

(6) The Myth of Japan as a Mono-Racial Country

In September 1986, Yasuhiro Nakasone, the Prime Minister of Japan, made a speech, which was "intended solely for Japanese ears."[58] It was at a seminar of the leading Liberal Democratic Party to which he belonged. In his speech, the Prime Minister referred to the intellectual standard of the United States and said that it was low due to minority groups such as African-Americans and Hispanic immigrants. Only those in the Japanese mass media attended the seminar. When the American media picked up this comment, it created an international commotion and became controversial in the United States. Nakasone was pressed to explain what he meant in his speech, and he clarified that Japan is a mono-racial nation, and as such, it

---

[53] Sachiko Kibata. 2014. In Ito, Kinko. 2018. *Have You Heard about the Ainu? Part 2 Toward a Better Understanding and World Peace.* YouTube.

[54] Gӧran Therborn. 2006, p.7.

[55] Gӧran Therborn. 2006, p.7.

[56] Gӧran Therborn. 2006, p.23.

[57] ann-elise lewallen. 2016, p.5.

[58] Karel van Wolferen. 1989, p.267.

had been spared some of the social problems in education that multi-racial and ethnic nations such as the United States face. He also mentioned that no Japanese nationals who were a minority ethnic group received any discrimination.[59] According to Wolferen, "Judged by the context in which it is constantly used, 'homogeneity' is a code word for uniqueness" in Japan.[60] Nakasone's intention was "to stimulate ethnic pride among the public."[61] The Japanese government wrote in its 1980 report to the Human Rights Commission of the United Nations that there were no minority groups in Japan, and the administrators consider the idea of homogeneity very important.

The Ainu were very angry at Nakasone's assertion that Japan is a mono-racial nation, as were Japan's long time Korean and Chinese residents. The Kanto Utari Association, which consists of Ainu members living in the Tokyo metropolitan area, sent an open letter of inquiry to the Prime Minister on October 1, 1986. About a month later, an apology came in the form of a post card from Nakasone's agent. In it, he referred to the incident as a distortion of the Prime Minister's speech as reported by the mass media.[62] This led to many protest meetings among the Ainu and raised their awareness of persisting discrimination.

In 1994, Shigeru Kayano (1926 – 1998) became a representative in the House of Councilors of the Japanese Diet, the highest legislative organ. He was the first Ainu representative in the upper house and served until 1998. Thanks to many of his efforts, a new law called *Ainu Bunka Shinkō Hō* ("Law for the Promotion of the Ainu Culture and for the Dissemination and Advocacy for the Traditions of the Ainu and the Ainu Culture") was promulgated in May 1997. It was amended in 1999. The law aims at realizing a society where the Ainu people's ethnic pride is respected, where diverse cultures are developed within Japan, and where the knowledge is spread by educating Japanese citizens about the Ainu language, oral literature, music, dance, spirituality, and crafts. It was also in 1997 when the Japanese government established the Foundation for Research and Promotion of Ainu Culture (FRPAC) with two headquarters, one in Sapporo and the other in Tokyo, to promote Ainu language classes, festivals, and recitals[63]. The Law for the Promotion of the Ainu Culture and for the Dissemination and Advocacy for the Traditions of the Ainu and the Ainu Culture flatly denied the notion that Japan is a mono-racial nation. However, the new law did not refer to guaranteeing the Ainu's dignity and rights as the indigenous people. The Japanese government recognized the Ainu as the indigenous people of Japan only in 2008, and prejudice and discrimination is still a social issue for the Ainu of today[64].

Japan is a relatively racially and ethnically homogeneous country when compared with nations such as the United States, Canada, Great Britain, and Sweden. However, contrary to the notion that Japanese people are mono-racial, minorities such as Korean and Chinese residents live in modern Japan, as do naturalized members of other foreign countries. Their presence is partly due to Japan's colonial past that started with the annexation of Korea in 1910. It continued with a territorial expansion to East and Southeast Asia that lasted until the end of World War II. According to the recent statistics by the Ministry of Health, Labor, and Welfare, the rate of Japanese marrying foreigners has been at about 3.3% since 2013. In 2015, the majority of foreign

---

[59] FRPAC. 2010, p.10.
[60] Karel van Wolferen. 1989, p.267.
[61] Karel van Wolferen. 1989, p.267.
[62] Nobuyuki Ogasawara. 2004, pp.186-188.
[63] Barbara Poisson. 2002.
[64] Noriyuki Kurihara. 2017, pp.89-91.

spouses were from China, the Philippines, Korea, the United States, and Thailand. Due to international marriages, a newborn per 30 babies has a parent who is not native Japanese. The number of foreign workers in Japan increased by 70% in recent years. There were 1.22 million foreign workers in 1991, and in 2011, the number was 2.8 million[65].

There is also still a significant number of other minority group called *burakumin* in Honshu. The term literally means "hamlet people" whose ancestors descended from the occupational caste ("untouchables") of the Tokugawa Period (1603 – 1867). The term *burakumin* also included *Eta* ("full of filth"), *Hinin* ("non-humans"), and *yotsu* ("four-legged")[66]. The Tokugawa government's caste system was based on the Confucian ideology of productivity. It constituted the four castes and the untouchables, namely, the samurai, peasants, artisans, merchants, and the untouchables. The *burakumin* were emancipated as the feudal Tokugawa Era ended, and the new Meiji government began.

*Burakumin*s are racially the same as the Japanese but their ancestors engaged in businesses that dealt with dead flesh, either that of animals or humans, or entertainment. The occupational outcastes included gravediggers, makers and sellers of leather goods, executioners, lower-class itinerants, acrobats, jugglers, and beggars as well. The Meiji government emancipated this group in 1869[67], which was at about the same time that the slaves became free in the United States. There still exists much prejudice and discrimination against the *burakumin* in contemporary Japan regarding education, employment, housing, and marriage even though they look the same as other Japanese people.[68]

As compared with *burakumin*, the Ainu tend to look somewhat different from *Wajin* and they are discriminated in the same social arenas – in education, employment, and marriage. A *Wajin* woman from Honshu who married an Ainu man once told me over dinner, "In Hokkaido, there are no problems with the *burakumin* people. They are simply not here, and we do not think much about them, either. Instead, the *Wajin* people here say that Hokkaido has the Ainu problem. I have heard that some Ainu man married a woman from Honshu, and they live in a community where the Ainu are the majority. The wife is a *burakumin*, and she looks like a *Wajin*. The folks around here do not know or care about her *burakumin* status. I have experienced prejudice and discrimination because my husband is an Ainu and we live in an area where few Ainu people live. People in our community would not visit us or stop by, and it was very difficult to get along with my mother-in-law. I felt lonely. Anyway I think both the *burakumin* in Honshu and the Ainu in Hokkaido share the same kind of social problems."

Japan, a democratic country, looks more racially homogeneous than other countries. It has enjoyed a very long time of peace after WWII. However, it still seems to take time before every group can benefit from equal treatment and feels comfortable being open about their membership.

---

[65] www.mhlw.go.jp/toukei/saikin/hw/jinkou/tokushu/konin16/dl/01.pdf. Accessed 4/6/19.

[66] Karel van Wolferen.1989. Edwin O. Reischauer. 1990.

[67] Kato & Wakazono. 2018, p.68.

[68] Kenneth Henshall. 2011, p. 54. Edwin O. Reischauer. 1990, p.103.

Figure 7 The Ainu community center called Seikatsukan ("Living Hall") in Nibutani in Biratori Town. The Hokkaido prefectural government provides the facility with administrative and operational subsidies in an effort to preserve Ainu culture and provide consultation and guidance for the local residents.

Chapter 2: The History and the World of the Ainu in *GOLDEN KAMUY*

The popularity of *GOLDEN KAMUY*, a Japanese serialized manga by Satoru Noda, has added fuel to the fire of interest in the Ainu people and their traditions among high school students and young adults in Japan and abroad in recent years. The comic has been appearing in the *Weekly Young Jump* magazine since 2014, and it has sold millions of copies. Shueisha, one of the major publishing houses in Japan, issued more than 17 volumes of compiled episodes of *GOLDEN KAMUY*. The manga is now a very popular *anime* (Japanese animation) as well.

GOLDEN KAMUY takes place in the latter part of the Meiji Era (1868-1912) in Hokkaido. One of the major protagonists is Saichi Sugimoto, an ex-soldier who returned from the Russo-Japanese War (1904-1905). He is in desperate need of money in order to help a wife of Toraji, his now deceased best friend with whom he grew up. He promised Toraji to get a medical cure for his wife's eye diseases. Sugimoto moves from Tokyo to Hokkaido to make a fortune in one stroke. Another major protagonist is a young Ainu girl named *Asirpa*. The brave teenager is searching for her late father who had something to do with the gold bullion that the Ainu hid somewhere in Hokkaido.

In the first episode of *GOLDEN KAMUY*, Sugimoto and *Asirpa* meet in a wood when a brown bear tries to attack Sugimoto. *Asirpa* happens to be nearby and notices the incident. Being an excellent archer, she saves Sugimoto with her arrows. She explains about them to Sugimoto, "The poisonous arrows of the Ainu have a mixture of various ingredients to maximize the potency. Each family has its own secret recipes and transmit them from generation to generation." Noda, the author of the comics, tells his readers about Christian Bergmann's eco-geographical rule that animals living in Hokkaido such as bears, deer, squirrels, foxes, and rabbits, are bigger than those living in Honshu. The German biologist stated that among the same species, the size of those living in a colder environment are bigger.[69]

Asirpa teaches Sugimoto various Ainu traditions such as language, philosophy, religion, cuisine, clothing, customs and manners as well as survival skills in the wild as they travel through Hokkaido together. They become very good friends.[70] *GOLDEN KAMUY* depicts various aspects of the Ainu history and traditional Ainu life that many people do not know or have not cared enough to know in contemporary Japan. It is the very first Japanese comic that has an Ainu girl as one of the major protagonists. It portrays the Ainu and their lifestyle with very positive and powerful images. In this sense, this manga is a groundbreaking comic series that is also educational. It promotes understanding and contributes to eliminating prejudice, misunderstanding, and negative stereotypes.

The Ainu used to live harmoniously and peacefully in the *Ainu Mosir*, where land and natural resources were abundant since ancient times. They did not have a notion of private land ownership; it was for everyone. They led an eco-friendly life in a symbiotic relationship with nature.

The Ainu religion is animistic and polytheistic. There are specialized gods everywhere – in the fire, water, wind, earthquake, tsunami, thunder, and in other natural events. Other gods reside in things and buildings such as bowls, chopping boards, houses, and toilets. Still others are invisible and psychological such as sloth and lust. They believed that everything that exists in the world has its purpose given by the Divine. They are all equal in that they have precious lives.

---

[69] Satoru Noda. 2018. *GOLDEN KAMUY*. Volume 1.

[70] Noriyuki Kurihara. 2017, pp.6-15.

The Ainu lived in harmony with nature as hunters, gatherers, anglers, and limited farmers. They had a tremendous amount of knowledge about nature and its cycles because their livelihood depended on it. They took only whatever was necessary from their surroundings – berries, nuts, mushrooms, grasses, salmon, deer, arctic hares, and foxes. They never overharvested or overhunted.

Figure 8 A building called *pu* where the Ainu traditionally stored grains and other food. This *pu* is exhibited between the Ainu Cultural Museum and the Historical Museum of Saru River in Nibutani in Biratori Town (2012).

The Ainu lived in a *kotan* (community) that is usually located very close to a river which provided them with water and salmon, their staple. They constructed a house called *cise* made of all natural materials available in each region such as trees, grass, and vines. They used no nails to build a *cise* (traditional Ainu houses with thatched roofs).[71]

Figure 8 Several reconstructed *cises* (traditional Ainu houses with thatched roofs) in Nibutani. Currently the Fire Law prohibits construction of *cise* for residence.

[71] Ainu Minzoku Hakubutsukan. 2009.

Figure 9 Inside one of the traditional Ainu houses in Nibutani. The fireplace is at the center of the house, and the residents worked and ate food around it. The Ainu respected the goddess of fire. At night, the elders would tell their children and grandchildren the Ainu legends and folktales.

The history of all hitherto societies is written by the ruling people and from their particular perspectives. Power, wealth, and privileges enable them to write it in any way they please. The class with the means of material production at their disposal can easily exert control over the means of mental production for the masses, which affects their worldviews on politics, ethics, religions, etc.[72] Many Japanese people still think wrongly that the history of Hokkaido started with the establishment of the Colonization Board in 1869. The new Meiji government began "developing" the land where the Ainu lived over so many years. Today's Hokkaido was known as Ezochi for a long time in Japan, and the history of Ezochi actually goes back to the Old Stone Age. The oldest ruin in Ezochi is located in Chitose City, and it is about 21,000 years old.[73] During the Jomon Period (13,000 B.C. – 500 B.C.), the people produced "mat-patterned pottery, which shows great variety, boldness, and originality in its designs."[74] The inhabitants of Ezochi lived in the same way as those Jomon people in Honshu (Japan's main island). The residents lived in pit-dwellings in a village and hunted deer and bears, and they cooked in pottery.

More technologically advanced Yayoi culture replaced or absorbed Jomon culture starting with the movement of people from Korea in the third century B.C. Rice cultivation and artifacts made of iron and bronze were introduced to the northern part of Kyushu, and it spread to central Japan and then to the Kanto Plain where Tokyo, today's capital of Japan, is located. The new era was called the Yayoi Period, and it lasted until 300 A.D.[75]

Interestingly, Yayoi culture did not reach Ezochi, and their old way of life from the Jomon Period continued even though the use of ironware was introduced. This period in Ezochi is called the Post Jomon Period because the traditional use of Jomon potteries continued. The period lasted between 300 B.C. and 700 A.D, and it corresponded to the Yayoi and Tumulus Periods in Honshu.[76] During the Satsumon Period (700 A.D. – 1300 A.D.), those inhabitants of Ezochi and the northern part of Tohoku utilized unglazed earthenware with the designs made by

[72] Karl Marx. 1964, p.78.
[73] Yoichi Tsunoda. 2018, p.216.
[74] Edwin O. Reischauer. 1990, p.10.
[75] Reischauer, Edwin O. 1990, p.10.
[76] Takuro Segawa. 2016, p. 18.

head bristles. Their abodes had a fireplace and a kitchen range. They lived in communities near the rivers and fished salmon and trout.[77]

The people who came down south from Sakhalin advanced to the northern tip of Ezochi and the coasts of the Okhotsk Sea toward the end of the Post Jomon Period. The Nivkh (formerly known as the Gilyak), who now live in the northern part of Sakhalin, are considered to be their descendants.[78] The Okhotsk culture coexisted with the Post Jomon Period and the following Satsumon Period between the fifth and the 9th centuries.

The Okhotsk culture is considered to have originated in China and Sakhalin, and it covered Sakhalin, the northern part of Ezochi, and the southern Kuril Islands. The Okhotsk people engaged in fishing herrings and Okhotsk Atka mackerels. They also hunted Steller sea lions, sea lions, seals, and fur seals to make a living. They grew grains like millet, and domesticated pigs and dogs. They traded with the Tungus and the Japanese in northern Honshu. After the 7th century, the Okhotsk people advanced to the Kuril Islands, and they started to have conflicts with the Satsumon people.[79] The Okhotsk people eventually moved to Sakhalin after the 10th century when the Satsumon people started to seek salmon fishery all over Ezochi. The Satsumon people eventually absorbed those Okhotsk people who remained in Ezochi by the 13th century.[80]

After the end of the Satsumon Period, came an era called "the Ainu Cultural Period." It lasted until 1868 when the Tokugawa Period (1600 – 1867) ended and the new Meiji Government began. The traditional Ainu culture reached its maturity between the 12th and 13th centuries, which corresponds to Kamakura Period (1185 – 1333 A.D.) in Honshu. In contemporary Japan, the Ainu people occasionally use the traditional equipment and clothes from the era for formal occasions and ceremonial and religious rituals. *GOLDEN KAMUY* depicts and explains these clothes such as *cikarkarpe* and *attus* in some detail on the cover of certain volumes.

During the "Ainu Cultural Period," the Ainu started to live in flat-style houses with thatched roofs (*cise*) and dress themselves in *attus*, the elaborately embroidered clothes made of elm tree fiber with the Ainu motifs and designs. They used sake and utilized *inaw* (a sacred shaved wood stick for religious rites and ceremonies given to gods) and lacquerwares for religious rituals and purposes.

The "Ainu Cultural Period" was also the time when vigorous trading took place between the Ainu and the *Wajin* who advanced to the southern part of Ezochi. The areas of the trade for the Ainu stretched from the northeastern China, Kamchatka Peninsula, the Aleutian Islands, the downstream reaches of the Amur River, and Japan (Akita, Hirosaki, etc.).[81] The Ainu traded goods such as Steller's sea eagle feathers and food (smoked salmon, *kombu* [kelp], etc.), fur, Chinese money, and pottery with Japanese goods in Honshu. Immigrants came to Ezochi from Honshu, and they brought items such as wooden bowls, chopsticks, kitchen stoves, weaving devices, as well as their religious beliefs.[82]

---

[77] Yoichi Tsunoda. 2018, p. 218.

[78] Segawa, Takuro. 2016, p.19.

[79] Kato & Wakazono. 2018, p.18, Tsunoda, Yoishi. 2018, p. 222, Uemura, Hideaki. 2008, pp.18-19.

[80] Segawa, Takuro. 2016, pp. 19-20, Tsunoda, Yoichi. 2018, p.218.

[81] Takuro Segawa. 2007.

[82] Tsunoda, Yoichi. 2018, pp.224-225, Uemura, Hideaki. 2008, pp.26-27.

Figure 10 My host father is wearing *attus*, a traditional Ainu clothing made of elm tree fiber and appliqued with cotton cloths and elaborate embroidery.

Figure 11 *Iyoikiri*, a place in an Ainu home where treasures are stowed and shown including lacquered wares that stored food for rituals and grains. They were obtained by trading with the Wajin (Photo by the author: courtesy of Kayano Shigeru Nibutani Ainu Shiryokan).

Ezo and Ezochi are former names for today's Hokkaido. They are used interchangeably, but Ezo also refers to the native inhabitants of Ezochi. *Chi* literally means "the earth," "land," "a spot," "the ground," "a place," and "the soil".[83] The word Ezo appears in *Kojiki*, the oldest historical chronicle of Japan, which dates back to the year 712. The term also appears very often in *Nihon Shoki* and other historical records such as *Shoku Nihongi*, *Nihon Kōki*, and *Shoku Nihon Kōki*, which were published between 720 and 901. Historically, the Chinese used the term Ezo as a derogatory name for the barbarians who did not belong to the Han clan. In ancient Japan, the central government used the term Ezo (also Emishi) to refer to the people in the northeast who would not subjugate themselves to the Yamato. Later the term Ezo became a Japanese expression that refers to the Ainu people only.[84]

There have been many theories about who the Ezo really were since the days of Hakuseki Arai (1657 – 1725) and Norinaga Motoori (1730 – 1801), who were well-known scholars during the Tokugawa Period. During the Meiji period, anthropologists and archaeologists came up with

[83] Nakajima, Fumio. 1993, p. 76.
[84] Kojima, Kyoko. 2009, pp.14-18.

their own theories as well as those who studied the Ainu names of various places. However, there is not a definite theory that explains the relationship between the Ezo and the Ainu.

The Japanese claimed Ezo in the 15th century, and a substantial increase in *Wajin* immigration to Ezochi took place. It started to threaten the Ainu's peaceful way of living. The Matsumae Domain was located at the tip of Oshima Peninsula in the southernmost part of Ezochi. They could not grow rice to sustain their obligations, and the central Tokugawa Shogunate allowed and encouraged them to trade with the Ainu. In the 16th century, the Matsumae Port was thriving as a great trading port. The Ainu traders had also been doing successful business with Russia and China. They also brought dried salmon and herrings as well as skins of sea otters and sea lions from the eastern part of Ezochi and the Kuril Islands to the port. The traders brought the same kind of products from the northern part of Ezochi and Sakhalin as well as the gorgeous silk textiles from China called *Ezonishiki*. They were of great value and usefulness. More than 300 ships from Japan came to trade at the Matsumae Port in Ezochi.[85]

The Matsumae Domain was located in the southern part of Ezochi, but it was in the farthest north as compared with other Domains of Japan. Their finances depended on trading with the Ainu since they could not grow rice like other domains. Matsumae was a bustling place where the Ainu freely traded with the *Wajin* in Ezochi as well as across the Tsugaru Strait to northern Honshu. The Matsumae Domain wanted to monopolize trading with the Ainu and prohibited other domains. The domain established facilities for trading and commercial posts along the coastal lines and let the samurai run them. Starting in the 1710s, the Matsumae Domain called the posts, where fish were caught, *basho*. *Basho* literally means "a place." The Tokugawa government gave the Matsumae Doman permission to give the *Wajin* merchants trading rights in exchange for money. They thought that the money would stabilize the Domain's finances.

Merchants were much better at managing and creating profits than the samurai were. However, this new practice led to many merchants from faraway places advancing to all areas of Ezochi. They were interested in making maximum profits by shipping and trading merchandises. Many *Wajin* managers happened to have problems dealing with the Ainu in a humanitarian manner. Long hours of labor and violence were normal part of their management, and the exploitation escalated. At the beginning of this *basho* system, the merchants used to go back to Esashi, Matsumae, and Hakodate to spend the winters at the end of the fishing season. Later, they started to remain in their *basho* and forced the Ainu to work as laborers year-round. This changed the Ainu's means of earning a living from hunting, fishing, and gathering to wage laborers.[86]

The *Wajin* merchants' exploitative and violent trading practices instituted harsh realities for the Ainu. They forced not only adults but also children to work for them. They kidnapped the Ainu who were able to work from their *kotan* and forced them to work as anglers and laborers. They caught herrings and made them into fertilizers for commercial crops such as cotton and indigo grown in Tokyo, Osaka, and Kyoto. Other seafood such as dried kelp, sea slug, and abalones were exported to China.

The Ainu were overworked in labor camps located in faraway places, and they could go home only once in several years. They missed their loved ones back home. The *Wajin* merchant-managers treated the Ainu laborers like human cattle in order to increase efficiency of production. Many of laborers died of starvation and malnutrition as well as from extremely cold winters. The workers ate only one bowl of rice or leftover rice gruel per day, that is, if the *Wajin* left anything

[85] Uemura, Hideaki. 2008, p.29.

[86] Uemura, Hideaki. 2008, p.33. Tsunoda, Yoichi. 2018, p. 236. FRPAC. 2012, p.5.

after they finished eating. When the Ainu workers became sick, the *Wajin* bosses provided no medicine. The Japanese subcontractor merchants segregated the Ainu men and women of workable and marriageable age in different communities. They also made Ainu women their objects of sexual abuse making them their "local wives," which functioned as a substitute for legal prostitution. The Ainu had not been immune to diseases such as syphilis, smallpox, and other illnesses that the new immigrants brought to their land. The epidemics led to massive depopulation. The Ainu protested against the harsh treatment by the *Wajin*, who suppressed them easily.[87]

During the 18th century the Russians started to frequent the shores of northern Japan looking for ice-free ports to expand its territories. Other nations were also interested in the strategic location of Hokkaido. The Tokugawa government recognized that it was imperative to incorporate the *Ainu Mosir* into Japanese territory as soon as possible and make the Ainu Japanese nationals by forced assimilation. The officials considered the Ainu as "undeveloped" or "barbaric," and the Ainu ended up losing their human rights and freedom.[88] Kikuchi Isao, a Japanese professor of history, states that it was very unfortunate that the government audaciously considered that the Ainu would benefit from the assimilation policies by transitioning from being primitive to becoming civilized.[89]

Further exploitation of the Ainu and their homes took place when the Tokugawa Shogunate co-opted Ezochi in 1799 and 1807 in order to capitalize on the international shipping trade. The Russians were interested in ice-free ports in Ezochi, and their vessels started to frequent the shores in the 18th century. The Tokugawa Shogunate sensed a crisis about these Russian explorers. The Shogunate claimed Ezochi a foreign land that did not belong to any world powers, and it could not leave the Domain of Matsumae in charge of this land. There was a fear that the Ainu people might ally with the foreign powers and leave Japan.

In 1786, Shihei Hayashi (1738-1793), a samurai in Sendai, published *Sangoku Tsūran Zusetsu*. It was a book on geography, and Hayashi advocated the necessity of Japanese coastal defense. He stated that the nation needed to pay more attention to its three closest neighbors surrounding it, namely, Korea, Ryūkyū (Okinawa), and Ezochi (Hokkaido) to establish trade and military defenses, especially against Russia. Hayashi especially urged the government to obtain Ezo as Japanese territory.[90] The Tokugawa government put the Eastern part of Ezochi under its direct control in 1799, and the Western part in 1807 in order to capitalize on the international shipping trade. Hayashi's book evidences his beliefs about Ezochi, and it suggests wide opinion and policy.

Ezochi was located between northern Honshu and Russia, and it definitely occupied a strategic location for national and international security. We must know the status of the world, especially colonization by the several world powers, in order to understand why Japan was interested in Ezochi at the end of the Edo Period (1603 – 1867).

Great Britain, which had the first Industrial Revolution, started its colonization in Africa and advanced to East Asia: India's Mughal Empire became a colony, and China lost the Opium War and colonization began. France advanced to Indochina after the French Revolution in 1789. The colonial expansion took place in the middle of the 19th century. Japan was next to be

---

[87] Kayano, Shigeru. 2009, pp.35-47. lewallen, ann-elise. 2016, pp.132-133.
[88] Uemura, Hideaki. 2008, pp.3-4.
[89] Kikuchi, Isao. 2002, p.244.
[90] Uemura, Hideaki. 2008, p.38.

colonized by Great Britain, France, or Holland from the west, by the Russians from the north, and the United States from the east.[91]

The Americans were interested in Japanese ports where their steamships could take refuge, take on water, and be resupplied with coal. However, Japan's self-imposed national isolation policy of the time prohibited it. Not only the Americans but also the British and Russians sent expeditions to Japan in their efforts to open their ports to foreign ships. In July 1853, a large fleet of "black ships" led by Commodore Matthew C. Perry entered Uraga Bay (today's Tokyo Bay), which was nothing but a surprise to the Japanese. Perry brought a letter from the U.S. president demanding opening of the country and starting trade relations.[92] It was also in 1853 when Toshiakira Kawaji, a representative of the Tokugawa government, and Yevfimiy Putyatin, an admiral in the Imperial Russian Navy representing Russia, started to negotiate the national borders in Nagasaki. It was Japan's very first negotiation with a foreign nation. Kawaji argued that the Ainu were people belonging to Japan, and thus the land where they lived is a Japanese territory.[93] With all these foreign threats, Japan had to act quickly to show to the world that Ezochi was indeed its national land.

At the beginning of the Meiji Period (1868 – 1912), the new Meiji Government abolished the feudalistic caste system of the Tokugawa society, which prohibited the samurai, farmers, artisans, and merchants from moving from one caste to another. For example, individuals of different castes could not marry each other in the strict closed system. The government also emancipated the outcastes, the untouchables such as *eta* ("full of filth") and *hinin* ("non-humans")[94] in August 1869. These derogatory terms were used for occupational castes who engaged in certain "unclean" jobs such as digging graves, tanning leather, and being entertainers in a society that was primarily vegetarian and made up of Buddhists. With the abolishment of the system, everyone became *de jure* equal. However, the descendants of the untouchables are still discriminated against in the 21st century Japan, which is a persistent social problem of injustice and inequality.

The Meiji government enacted the Family Registration Law in 1869 and incorporated the Ainu and their land into Japan. They became "ordinary" Japanese citizens with their newly created Japanese surnames. However, the Family Registration Law classified the Ainu as former natives, and it led to a new kind of social discrimination. The policies regarding the registration included termination of certain Ainu customs and manners, and the Ainu were encouraged to learn the Japanese language. The Ainu were traditionally hunting and gathering people. They also engaged in limited farming at home and gathered mountain vegetables. The new government forced them to engage in agriculture and abandon their traditional lifestyle. Many Ainu did not make successful farmers. Many others died from famines in the 1880's, and the population dwindled.[95]

The Japanese government directly controlled Hokkaido from 1869 when the Hokkaido Colonization Board was established. The government institutionalized and normalized the exploitation of the Ainu. The Japanese government encouraged mainland people to immigrate to Hokkaido in great numbers, which contributed to population growth. The government supported the new immigrants by granting them travel money, housing, food, and agricultural equipment.

---

[91] Ooyama, 1992, p.2. Reischauer, Edwin O. 1990, pp.94 – 95.
[92] Edwin O. Reischauer. 1990, p.95.
[93] Uemura, Hideaki. 2008, pp.40-41.
[94] Kato and Wakazono. 2018, p.68.
[95] Kato & Wakazono. 2018, p.68, Uemura, Hideaki. 2008, pp.45-46.

The *Wajin* stole the land where the Ainu once lived harmoniously and peacefully, and confiscated their natural resources. Unfortunately, the Ainu did not have a concept of private land ownership, and the new immigrants felt they were entitled to own the land occupied by the Ainu.

The natural habitat that enabled the Ainu to lead a unique way of life decayed rapidly due to development and over-harvesting. Tomeji Kaizawa, one of my Ainu informants, told me during the filming of his interview that the Ainu appreciates everything that exists in nature. The Ainu go to the mountains and fields and give thanks to the gods first for the opportunity when harvesting. They reap whatever amount is necessary and never over-harvest. They always leave some for the following year so that they can benefit from nature again. The Ainu lives in harmony with nature, but the *Wajin* were more interested in their own business and profit. They took the best fertile land from the Ainu and exploited it.[96]

The Japanese government promulgated "the Hokkaido Former Aborigines Protection Act," which had 13 articles, on March 2 in 1899. The term "former aborigines" suggests that it was an unlawful invasion. It was also an insult to the Ainu. The Ainu, who became commoners, obtained their "new" land that was often arid and not suitable for agriculture. The Japanese immigrants took all the good and fertile land. The Articles of "the Hokkaido Former Aborigines Protection Act" are as follows:

<u>Article 1</u> - The government encourages the Ainu to engage in agriculture. Those who want to become a farmer will be given free land.
<u>Article 2</u> - Transfer of the land is prohibited unless it is inherited. Various taxes will be exempt for 30 years.
<u>Article 3</u> - If the land is not cultivated within 15 years, it will be confiscated.
<u>Article 4</u> - Those impoverished Ainu will be provided with farming tools and seeds.
<u>Article 5</u> - Those who get sick and cannot afford treatment will be given money for medication.
<u>Article 6</u> - Those who need assistance for various reasons will be assisted and for the deceased the fee for burial will be provided.
<u>Article 7</u> - Provision of tuition for the children of poverty.
<u>Article 8</u> -The expenses for (4) and (7) above will be paid from "Hokkaido Former Aborigines Joint Assets" and if more is needed, the money will come from the national treasury.
<u>Article 9</u> - Establishment of elementary schools for the Ainu
<u>Article 10</u> - Provisions in regard to the "Hokkaido Former Aborigines Joint Assets."
<u>Articles 11, 12, and 13</u> - State provisions of penalties and terms of operation.[97]

This law was not applied to all the Ainu equally. The conditions and standards of living differed much in various regions, and there were variations among the Ainu themselves. Some were financially independent, and others did not live in an Ainu community. Yet some others had been already engaging in agriculture. Many Ainu were poor when this law went into effect. Others wanted to seek various ways of making a living in areas other than agriculture. An increasing amount of exogamy took place between the Ainu and *Wajin* (non-Ainu ethnic Japanese). There were those who did not consider themselves as Ainu and lived just like any other *Wajin*. It was getting difficult to group together those people as one distinctive group.

The Japanese government obviously wanted not only the *Wajin* immigrants but also the Ainu to contribute to the development of Hokkaido by enforcing "the Hokkaido Former Aborigines Protection Act." The adaptation and changing the life style to farming was a very

---

[96] Tomeji, Kaizawa. 2015. *Have You Heard about the Ainu? Elders of Japan's Indigenous People Speak.* YouTube.
[97] Fumoto. 2008, pp.8-9.

difficult endeavor for many Ainu. The Meiji government made the land where the Ainu were living its national land in 1877 and distributed it among individuals who were willing to pay. However, the land the government provided to the Ainu was not suitable for agriculture.[98] In addition, they were not familiar with farming techniques, and the administrators did not give enough consideration for the application of the law, either. Many Ainu quit farming, and the new Japanese immigrants used their land. In addition, epidemics emerged, and the Ainu became very poor.[99] The Japanese government abolished "The Hokkaido Former Aborigines Protection Act" in 1997, which was 98 years after its promulgation.

The assimilation policy of the Colonization Board aimed at the Ainu's extinction by stripping them of not only land ownership but also identities, ways of life, language, religious practices, customs and manners, and spirituality, all of which have been very dear to the Ainu. For example, they had to abandon their traditional styles of hairdos and clothes and wear those of Japanese starting in 1798. This assimilation policy was part of an attempt to show to the world, especially Russia, that the Ainu are indeed Japanese, and thus, Ezochi, the land where they live, belonged to Japan.

The mandatory assimilation program was a process of ethnic cleansing that continued through the 19th and 20th centuries. The Ainu had their human rights taken away as an ethnic group in many ways in their native land. The greedy *Wajin* settlers in Hokkaido engaged in reckless hunting, fishing, and deforestation, which destroyed the natural resources that had enabled the Ainu's traditional way of life which was eco-friendly and self-sufficient. There were other Ainu traditions that the new government destroyed in its process of what is termed "mandatory assimilation."

The Family Registration Law enacted in 1869 made all Ainu people Japanese commoners, which meant they had to acquire Japanese surnames.[100] According to Shigeru Kayano, the Ainu did not have family names. The Meiji Government officials went to *kotan*s (Ainu communities) to provide them with new Japanese family names to register in the new government's family/census records. The names given to the Ainu had something to do with topographic characteristics, particular things, or events that took place. Some of the most common names are Hiranuma, Kaizawa, Kawakami, Kawanano, Kayano, Kurokawa, Kimura, Yoshikawa, and Nebesawa.[101] Some officials who came to Biratori Town were easy-going drunkards. Instead of working on creating names, they spent most of their time drinking at the inns where they were staying. The deadline came up soon enough. The officials created family names randomly such as Nitani and Kaizawa based on the geographical characteristics such as mountains, rivers, and brooks where they lived. Thus, the Ainu people who had the same last name are not necessarily related to one another by blood.[102]

During my trip to Biratori Town in 2011, I learned, to my surprise, that the Ainu people can still be identified by their last names. Here in the United States, one can surmise, to a certain degree, another's ethnicity and his or her ancestor's place of origin from their last names. This is socially significant regarding the decisions made in the recruitment process for scholarships and employment.

---

[98] FRPAC. 2012, p.7.

[99] Kono. 2002, pp.129-135.

[100] Uemura. 2008, pp. 45-46.

[101] Private conversation with Kazunobu Kawanano, 5/3/2011.

[102] Private conversation. 5/3/2011.

As for the meanings of the Ainu surnames listed above, Kaizawa means "a swampland where shellfish grow," Kawakami means "up the river," and Kurokawa means "a black river." Mr. Kawanano, one of my informants, said, "Some people's last name is Hirame. It means 'flounder.' It derives from an event in which a tsunami washed up many flounders near the ocean a long time ago. Thus, the Ainu who lived in the community got the family name Hirame."[103] The officials also wrote Ainu men's names in *katakana* characters and women's names in *hiragana* in the family registration papers.[104]

The official notice issued by the Colonization Board in 1871 included the policies of incorporating the Ainu into the Japanese family registration system and its forced assimilation. It prohibited the Ainu women's tattoos. It was a custom to put tattoos on girls in puberty around their mouths, on the back of their hands, and arms up to their elbows. Usually, the girls got their first tattoo between the age of 12 and 16, and their tattooing process ended by the time they got married. Traditionally, the Ainu considered women's tattoos beautiful.[105] Kato & Wakazono state, "To the Ainu women, their tattoos were their pride and their ethnic identity."[106]

The Ainu asked a calm and experienced woman to mark the girl's skin with tattoos. She would prepare disinfectant by boiling *yomogi* (mugwort) and the bark of *hannoki* (alder) and *yachidamo* (fraxinus mandschurica). The tattooing woman would disinfect the area, whether around the mouth or the arm or hand, first and scratch it with a sharp knife or a peace of sharp stone called *kokuyōseki* (obsidian). Then she would rub soot obtained from burning a bark of a birch tree or indigo dye obtained from trading with the *Wajin*. She disinfected the area again when the procedure was over. The colors faded as time passed by, and the tattoos were maintained by inking them every five years or so.[107]

Some girls had the tattoos all at once and others had it done in installments. The tattoos indicated that the Ainu girl is an adult, and she can now marry or participate in ceremonies. The Ainu also believed that the women could not go to heaven when they die unless they are tattooed. Thus, every Ainu woman had tattoos before the prohibition by the government.

My Ainu friend Fumiko told me that she used to see a few old Ainu women with their tattoos in her neighborhood during the Showa Period (1926 – 1989). I became her friend thanks to her father who was one of my informants when I visited the town in 2012 and 2014. Fumiko said to me when we had a cup of green tea together, "These old Ainu women seemed very scary. I was only a child in those days. Their tattoos around their mouths were supposed to be beautiful, but to me, I thought that they looked like monsters. There was a house with a few persimmon trees in our community. The orange colored persimmon fruits ripen in the fall, and they taste very good. They are sweet and nice. My friends and I saw that many ripe persimmons were left on the higher branches because the old woman could not reach them. We wanted to get them. Why not, right? They will get rotten, fall to the ground, and become a waste. So, we climbed up the tree and tried to get them. Then, this old woman with a big tattoo around her mouth dashed out of her house with a broom, yelled at us, and tried to chase us away. That was a very scary moment. We had never expected that! The old woman was born in the Meiji Period, but she had tattoos."[108]

---

[103] Private conversation. 5/3/2011.

[104] Kayano, Shigeru. 2009, pp.57-58.

[105] Tsunoda, Yoichi. 2018, p.206.

[106] Kato & Wakazono. 2018, p.69.

[107] Tsunoda, Yoichi. 2018, pp.206-207.

[108] Private conversation. June, 2012.

The assimilation policies also prohibited the Ainu men from wearing earrings.[109] The Ainu were required to learn and use the Japanese language, both oral and written. The official notice from the Sapporo Headquarters of the Colonization Board in 1876 indicated that the Ainu customs must be discarded and those who violated the assimilation policies would be severely punished. The notice from the Nemuro Branch of the Board in 1876 also ordered the Ainu to use their new Japanese names and not their original Ainu names. Kato and Wakazono state, "(This) is nothing but the negation of Ainu's unique traditional culture."[110]

In 1870, the government prohibited the Ainu from fishing salmon in the river using their traditional method. When I visited *Poroto Kotan* in Shiraoi in May 2011, one of the museum staff members kindly took me on a tour or the museum. He showed me various items regarding traditional Ainu lifestyle and gave me much information to introduce me to Ainu history and culture. We came to an area of the Ainu food exhibit, and he said to me, "Salmon was an Ainu staple just like rice is to the *Wajin*. Prohibition of catching salmon meant 'Death to the Ainu.'" I noticed tears welling up in his eyes as he talked to me.[111]

Salmon are large tasty fish that come back to their native rivers to lay eggs in fall, when the Ainu must start storing food for cold winters. The Ainu call salmon *kamuycep*, or "Gods' fish". The gods provide the Ainu with the fish to eat, but they made them into clothes and shoes. The Ainu offered a religious prayer ritual to the gods of the river and water when the salmon fishing season neared. We should note here that salmon is not just food, but it is closely related to the Ainu's religious worldview. They believe that the gods drop salmon from heaven to the ocean, and the fish go upstream to enrich the lives of the Ainu. The Colonization Board did not have any regard or respect for the Ainu's traditional way of life.[112]

In 1876, the government banned the traditional poisonous arrows and spring-loaded poison traps for hunting. The poison was derived from *aconite*, a beautiful wild flower, and each Ainu family possessed a carefully guarded recipe. The Meiji government totally prohibited the Ainu from hunting deer in 1889, which led to more dire living conditions for the minority group. Deer had been an indispensable part of Ainu everyday life. Its meat was a very important source of nutrition, and the Ainu used its skin not only for trading but also as a raw material for making warm winter clothes and various tools and devices. They used its horn for digging earth and its bones for arrow points.[113] The Ainu preserved deer by slaughtering the animal and splitting the meat thinly and hanging it to dry outside of the house. Another method entailed boiling and drying the meat. When the meat is almost dry, the Ainu people bring it inside the house and dry it on the hanging shelf over the fireplace. They then smoke the meat to preserve it. They stored the meat either in the house or in *pu* ("storage for food and other important items").[114] Deer became an easy resource for money making for immigrants, and its population was facing extinction by the middle of the Meiji Period (1868 – 1912). For example, they hunted about 76,000 deer in 1875.

These prohibitions were nothing but a death sentence to the Ainu especially because salmon and deer were their staple foods. They would become a criminal in their own backyard if they were to fish or hunt. The land was a place where their ancestors lived for many years, but

---

[109] Ainu Minzoku Hakubutsukan. 2009, pp.190-191.

[110] Kato & Wakazono. 2018, p.68.

[111] 2015. *Have You Heard about the Ainu? Elders of Japan's Indigenous People Speak.* YouTube.

[112] Ainu Minzoku Hakubutsukan. 2009, pp.65-66, Tsunoda, Yoichi. 2018, pp.94-95.

[113] Ainu Minzoku Hakubutsukan. 2009, p.62.

[114] Ainu Minzoku Hakubutsukan. 2009, p.108.

the Japanese government confiscated mountains, swamplands, and wilderness. The Ainu were strongly encouraged to engage in other businesses. Many Ainu did not make great farmers, and they suffered from recurring famines in the 1880s.[115] Their population fell due to poverty and starvation. They also suffered from epidemics of the new diseases brought by the Japanese immigrants and to which they did not have immunity, such as smallpox, tuberculosis, and syphilis. The Ainu also had a lower standard of living compared with that of *Wajin* and suffered from malnutrition. Single people increased, and forced abortion added to the decreasing birth rate. The Ainu population rapidly declined from the beginning of the 19th century until the end of the Tokugawa Period (1600 – 1867).[116]

One of the social reforms during the Meiji Period (1868 – 1912) included drawing up the new constitution. It was "a gift from the emperor to his people" and was promulgated on February 11, 1889. The government hoped to impress "the West with Japan's progress toward 'civilization'."[117] It guarantees compulsory education, and Ainu children were provided with an education that included learning both oral and written Japanese. The forced assimilation policy forbid them to use their own language. The Sapir-Whorf hypothesis, or the language relativity thesis, points out that the language one speaks influences one's worldview. It affects the way one thinks, interacts, and perceives the reality. The imposition of the Japanese language meant that the Ainu people would lose their unique worldview. The Ainu children went to school along with the *Wajin* children at the beginning of the colonization process. It was quite a burden for them to learn Japanese, their new language, and the school attendance was low. According to the Hokkaido *Kyūdojin* (Ex-natives) Protection Law, the government built Ainu Schools (*Kyūdojin* Schools), in the communities that had more than 30 school age children. In 1907, twenty-one such schools were built. The mandatory courses included ethics, Japanese, arithmetic, physical education, farming (for boys), and sewing (for girls). They did not teach geography, history, or science. The Ainu children were thought to be inferior to *Wajin* children, and their curriculum was differentiated from that of *Wajin* children.[118]

Private Ainu schools established by English Christian missionaries such as John Batchelor (1854 – 1944) and Lucy Payne were quite successful and played an important role in Ainu education. The schools inspired the administrators to come up with the original public school curricula for the Ainu children. Their school attendance increased to 90% after the 1910s.[119]

The school segregation lasted until 1937. A few of the Ainu elders I interviewed attended desegregated schools. They told me that not only the non-Ainu Japanese students but also the teachers and principals bullied and ridiculed them at school. Many of the Ainu children were so poor, and they did not bathe or change their clothes as often as other children did. The Japanese children made fun of them as being stinky or for the contents of their lunch boxes. Fukuji Kaizawa still remembered very vividly how his female *Wajin* homeroom teacher persistently bullied him at his junior high school after so many years. He said, "It persisted so much that I quit going to junior high school. If I had not had that nasty teacher, my life would have been very different."[120]

---

[115] Uemura. 2008, p.46, Kato & Wakazono. 2018, p.75.

[116] Kato & Wakazono. 2018, p.83, Namikawa, Kenji. 2010, p.68.

[117] Reischauer, Edwin O. 1990, pp.122-123.

[118] Kato & Wakazono, 2018, p.94.

[119] Kato & Wakazono. 2018, p.98.

[120] Private conversation 2012

Chapter 3: My Ainu Connection

It was during my childhood in Japan when my first contact with anything Ainu took place. In 1962, my uncle, my father's elder brother, who lived with my grandparents and used to work for the Japan Railways (JR), gave his parents a gift of free train tickets to Hokkaido. He wanted them to visit their friends, do sightseeing, and relax in hot springs on the northern island.

One day my father said to my mother when he came home from work, "I've decided to take a week off and escort my parents to Hokkaido. I don't want them to get lost and end up in Sakhalin!"

"What are you talking about!?" my mother laughed.

"Sakhalin is very close to Hokkaido, yet it is a Russian territory now. You cannot take a train there!" she said. I am sure my father just wanted to be funny.

My mother was a principal at a municipal kindergarten with a few hundred children aged five and six, and she was pregnant with my brother at the time. She was not too happy about the timing of their trip.

"Who is going to help me with little Kinko?" My mother said to my father anxiously.

"You are a strong and smart person, a career woman! You can take care of any situation just fine," my father replied.

On the morning of July 22, 1962, my father and grandparents began their trip to Hokkaido. They first took an express train from Nagoya to Tokyo for several hours. It was two years before the Tokaido Shinkansen Super Express started its service between Tokyo and Osaka in 1964, the year of the Tokyo Olympic Games. It was the very first Asian games. They enjoyed visiting Grandpa's sister for a day in the capital city. Then they took a night train to Aomori, where their train got on board a ferry connecting Honshu and Hokkaido. It took about four hours between Aomori and Hakodate.

It took many hours and different types of transportation to get to Hokkaido. It indeed was a very long trip. My father later told me that the sleeping car from Ueno (in Tokyo) to Aomori had three bunk beds with curtains on both sides of the aisles on the train. He slept in the top bed, Grandpa in the middle, and Grandma at the bottom where there was least swaying. My father also switched their cabin on the ship from second class to first class to provide his parents with more comfort.

My mother is the 11th and the last child in her family, and her father, who was 80 years old at the time, came to stay with us while my father was away. He was worried to death about my mother commuting to work on her bicycle with her huge abdomen. He would see my mother off at the gate, put his hands palm to palm, and pray that the baby would not come out while she was riding her bike! I was very happy my grandfather came to stay with us, but a week without Daddy seemed to be a very long time.

My grandparents' friends and their relatives were very nice and took them and my father to a few national parks and hot springs. They also invited them to stay in their homes. My father later told me when he was visiting me in Ohio that the scenery in the American Midwest reminded him of Hokkaido. Hokkaido was then quite different from central Honshu that had many metropolitan areas. My father and his parents were quite impressed with the beautiful, vast, and bucolic land with rich soil.

Figure 12 The house of one of my grandparents' friends in Hokkaido (Photo by Kunio Ito [1962]).

Figure 13 The friends and relatives of my grandparents are seeing them off. Hokkaido was so far away that it could have been their last "good-bye" (Photo by Kunio Ito [1962]).

Figure 14 Jigokudani (Hell Valley) in Noboribetsu, which is a well-known spa city. Many bubbling craters are the main source of thermal waters for the city's inns and hotels. Hot steam and water come from the volcanic activity. Hokkaido has many hot springs and scenic resort areas (Photo by Kunio Ito [1962]).

Figure 15 My grandparents at Jozankei Hot Springs in the Shikotsu Toya National Park (Photo by Kunio Ito [1962]).

Tourism to Hokkaido was becoming very popular and was a thriving economic driver in the region in the 1960s. The Ainu received national attention as part of this new interest in tourism, and many Ainu worked in the tourist industry. They performed with singing and dancing in shows for the *Wajin* (non-Ainu ethnic majority Japanese) tourists. Other Ainu people manufactured crafts and fabrics and sold souvenirs.[121]

When the Japanese travel for pleasure and for more than several days, their family members, relatives, friends, and co-workers give them *osenbetsu* (bon voyage cash gift). The travelers customarily bring local specialty foods and goods as *omiyage* (souvenir gifts) for those who gave them *osenbetsu*. Many tourists from Honshu (mainland Japan) poured into Hokkaido propelled by the Japanese tourism industry and purchased many Ainu artifacts such as woodcarvings, accessories, and traditional textile goods as well as seafood.

Figure 16 The author dressed in a traditional Ainu garment called *cijiri*[122] in a souvenir store owned by an Ainu man (2012). Women embroider traditional Ainu designs directly onto the cotton kimono.

[121] Shigeru Kayano. 2009, pp.154-156.

[122] In the eastern part of Hokkaido, *cijiri* is called *cikarkarpe*. Tsunoda, Yoichi. 2018, p. 149.

Figure 17 Items for sale in an Ainu souvenir shop: jackets with traditional Ainu motifs and embroidery, a vest made of animal skin, and woodcarvings (2012).

Figure 18 Many souvenir shops kept bear cubs in their storefronts in those days (Photo by Kunio Ito [1962]).

Shigeru Kayano (1926 – 2006), the first Ainu who was elected to the national assembly, described how he was involved with this tourism at that time in his book titled *Ainu no Ishibumi*. He was quite talented in woodcarving, opened a store in his native Nibutani (in Biratori Town), and made money. In order to support his family, Kayano also worked reluctantly in the tourism industry in Noboribetsu Hot Springs during the busy tourist season for several summers performing Ainu ceremonies, songs, and dances. He admitted that he did not really enjoy performing in front of the audience. To the Ainu, these ceremonies were sacred, and they were supposed to perform them only for certain occasions, and not every day for a show. Songs and dances are also for the enjoyment and bonding of the Ainu people; they are never for entertainment of the Japanese tourists from Honshu and other places.[123]

The money Kayano earned in the tourist business enabled him to purchase traditional Ainu folk artifacts, tools, and other items from the collectors. They were fast disappearing in the process of modernization, and collectors had been buying them up by visiting Ainu households. Many Ainu possessed these artifacts for their own collection as well. Kayano later opened a museum called Kayano Shigeru Nibutani Ainu Shiryōkan (Shigeru Kayano's Nibutani Museum

[123] Shigeru Kayano. 2009, p.154.

of Ainu Culture) to exhibit hundreds of Ainu folk artifacts he collected over the years. He was afraid that the traditional Ainu culture and their way of life would be long gone with the aging Ainu population, and he had an urge to record Ainu elders' voices, stories, and language for future generations.[124]

Kayano also pointed out that generally the ethnic majority Japanese are ignorant of or indifferent to the existence of the Ainu people, their customs and manners, religion, and the history of subjugation. I myself barely knew about them throughout my primary and secondary education in Honshu. My primary school teacher once told his 6th grade class that the Ainu lived in Hokkaido, but they did not live in reservations like some other indigenous people of the world. He also mentioned that the Ainu language does not have letters, and they transmitted their history, traditions, songs, religion, epics, and personal stories orally. That was all I remember.

In his book Kayano states that the *Wajin* tourists he encountered would ask him outrageous questions such as "What kind of food do you eat?" "Your Japanese is very good. Where did you learn it?" and "Do you pay taxes?" This kind of ignorance made Kayano become aware that the *Wajin* did not really understand the Ainu and their current situation at all. Kayano felt the need to explain and educate them about the history of the Ainu, the language, and customs and manners correctly.[125]

Now, back to my father's trip to Hokkaido.

My father and his parents really enjoyed the trip and brought back a small wooden jewelry box for me. It had a carved picture of two *kokeshi* dolls on the lid, and there was a mirror on the back of the lid. My cousin, who is 5 years older than I am and lived with my grandparents, received the same wooden box, which was larger. The other souvenirs that my father brought back included famous Hokkaido butter candies and three bears made from carved wood. They reminded me of a fairy tale about a bear family that my father used to read before bedtime. I learned that the Ainu men carved these souvenir bears, and my father placed them on the *tokonoma* (a recessed and decorative alcove) in our living room.

Figure 19 A woodcarving of a bear from an Ainu souvenir store.

Later my parents' friend visited Hokkaido and brought to our family a pair of wooden dolls. They were a husband and a wife dressed in traditional Ainu clothes, and my mother placed

[124] Shigeru Kayano. 2009, p.156.
[125] Shigeru Kayano. 2009.

them in a glass case on top of a chest of drawers. My father briefly explained about the Ainu, but I was too young to grasp who they really were.

Figure 20 Woodcarvings of an Ainu couple clad in traditional attire. The husband on the right is wearing a moustache and a beard. On his head is a *sapanpe*, a headdress for Ainu rituals. The wife on the left is wearing a *matanpus* on her hair and a *rektunpe* around her neck. A tattoo decorates her mouth area, which means that she is an adult.

I first met Shiro Kayano in Nibutani in Biratori Town on May 3, 2011. He is a tall and handsome man who is very friendly. He is the second son of the late and aforementioned Shigeru Kayano. Shiro graduated from a university, and he worked as his father's secretary in Tokyo between 1994 and 1998 when the elder Kayano served Japan's Diet (the highest legislative organ of the nation). Shiro is now the director of the cultural museum his father opened in Nibutani.

Figure 21 Shigeru Kayano's Nibutani Museum of Ainu Culture in Biratori.

Shiro said to me in my first interview that he wanted my students in the United States to know that the contemporary Ainu are totally assimilated into the mainstream Japanese culture. Their life is no different from that of *Wajin*. Shiro said, "The contemporary Ainu live in a modern house, eat Japanese food, drive cars and trucks, use computers and internet, and talk on the cell phone just like any other person in Japan today." He lamented, just like his late father, that many ethic majority Japanese do not know much about the Ainu, and ignorance and misunderstanding still prevail.[126]

Figure 22 Shiro Kayano at the entrance to the museum (2012).

Hokkaido is internationally famous for its abundant and beautiful nature with scenic mountains, bucolic fields, rivers, hot springs, and ski slopes. Shiretoko became a UNESCO World Heritage site in 2005.[127] Fishing, forestry, and farming are important industries of Hokkaido in which many Ainu work today. Other Ainu people engage in tourist businesses, working as guides and entertainers. They play musical instruments, sing, dance, and teach the general audience their culture and heritage at cultural festivals, cultural centers, and museums. Many are artists and artisans who sell their beautiful artwork to collectors, galleries, and tourists. Others have jobs just like anybody else; they work in city and town hall offices, transportation, excavation sites, convenience stores, restaurants, shops, and beauty salons.

Biratori is located in the southern central part of Hokkaido with a population of 5,116 as of August 2018.[128] The Town has 17 communities where many Ainu people live: Shiunkotsu, Saruba, Nina, Kawamukai, Kobira, Nibutani, Nioi, Osachinai, Horokeshi, Furenai, Niseu, Iwachishi, and Nukibetsu. In Nibutani, more than 70 % of residents are of Ainu descent. The *Wajin* are the minority in this particular community, and of course, this is very rare in Japan. Biratori is famous for dairy and agricultural products such as rice, tomatoes, potatoes, beef, and beans.[129]

[126] Private conversation with Shiro Kayano. 5/3/2011.
[127] www.worldheritagesite.org/list/Shiretoko. Accessed 1/26/19.
[128] www.town.biratori.hokkaido.jp/jinkou/toukei. Accessed 9/3/18.
[129] Ibid.

Figure 23 Beautiful nature is abundant in Hokkaido.

Figure 24 Biratori Beef is one of the special products of the town.

I did my fieldwork in Sapporo, Shiraoi, Shizunai, and Biratori in 2011, 2012, 2014, and 2018. Luckily, I was on my sabbatical during the spring semester of 2011 and the fall semester of 2018. During my trips to Hokkaido, I stayed in hotels and an inn owned by an Ainu couple as well as in the homes of kind and generous Ainu and *Wajin* people who opened their hearts to me.

Mr. Kazunobu Kawanano, an old Ainu man, told me when we arrived at his house on my first visit in 2011, "You are like our daughter, and you can consider us your parents. Feel free to ask us any questions or favors, and we will try our best to accommodate you." I stayed with the Kawananos several times, and we became very good friends, which made it very difficult to say "*Sayonara* (Good-bye)" at the end of each fieldwork.

A few other Ainu families let me stay in their homes in 2011, 2012, and 2014. Homestays provided me with rich, personal, and contextual data for my ethnography. Spending many hours with them as they went by their daily activities gave me an opportunity for direct, firsthand observations, provided me with precious experiences of Ainu ways of living, and offered me a much deeper insight into their social psychology.

Figure 25 The kitchen of one of my Ainu host families.

Figure 26 A typical Japanese breakfast cooked by my Ainu host mother with rice (Japanese staple) and miso soup. The other dishes include potatoes with pork, grilled fish, and sliced fresh tomatoes.

I interviewed more than three dozen people, both Ainu and *Wajin*, with structured and unstructured formats. I also took photographs and videotaped some of my interviewees, which became valuable visual and audio sources for my documentary films. Most scholars present their findings and data in a written format in an academic journal or a book, but I chose to do some of my presentations in the video format so that the audience can pick up more contextual information such as facial expressions, grunts, eye contacts, silence, postures, and gestures that are very important factors of non-verbal communication. A scholar cannot express them properly in a written form, and I definitely believe in the power of multimedia for both data gathering and presentation of the findings.

Chapter 4: Sabbatical (2011)

More than half a century had passed since my father brought me the wooden bears carved by the Ainu, a jewelry box, and sweets from his trip to Hokkaido. I was on my sabbatical during the spring semester of 2011, and my project entailed a trip to Hokkaido, learning about the Ainu by reading books and articles, and visiting several Ainu museums. Above all, I was going to meet the Ainu people for the first time! I was to get first-hand glimpses of the Ainu life: the people, their food, arts, crafts, and folk artifacts. The preparation for my trip to Hokkaido started a year earlier.

I contacted several Ainu research experts in Sapporo and other places and started to exchange e-mails with them regarding where I could start my research and the availability of resources at different Ainu centers and museums in Hokkaido. I had read several books by Shigeru Kayano, the first Ainu national Diet member who was bilingual in Ainu and Japanese, compiled and published a few Ainu-Japanese dictionaries, and provided help to Kyosuke Kindaichi, a famous Japanese professor and linguist regarding the Ainu language and its oral literature. Kayano is from the Nibutani area in Biratori Town, and he collected tools, devices, and clothes that the Ainu traditionally used in their everyday life and for formal occasions. He later opened his own museum called Shigeru Kayano's Nibutani Museum of Ainu Culture. I was fascinated by his books, which are full of descriptions about the Ainu history, language, traditions, family, oral literature, dances, songs, schools, jobs, religion, and experiences of the Ainu people. I went online and contacted the town asking if the staff members at the town's museums could provide me any help regarding my research. I also mentioned in my e-mail that I really wanted to meet the Ainu people. A young male staff member replied to my e-mail saying that he would be able to accommodate my needs. He also said that an Ainu man and his wife offered for me to stay at their home for a few days. He suggested that I call the man to arrange the home stay and gave me his cell phone number.

The Ainu man's name was Mr. Kazunobu Kawanano. He was born in 1934, and after he retired from his long career as a truck driver, he has been very active in the cultural events and festivals taking place in Biratori and elsewhere in Hokkaido as well as in Honshu. He was also involved with the preservation of Ainu culture and agriculture. Mr. Kawanano is friendly, helpful, and out-going as well as famous in town: everyone knows him. He lives with his wife Motoko after their six children married and left home. The couple have been hosting many researchers and professors at their home.

(1) My First Phone Call to an Ainu Man

I was really excited and anxious when I first made an international call to Mr. Kawanano from the United States. It was my very first time talking to an Ainu person. The following is how our conversation went.

His phone rings.

"*Moshi moshi!* (Hello!)" He answers cheerfully.

"Hello, my name is Kinko Ito. I am a professor of sociology. I am sure you have heard about me from the museum. I got your phone number from them."

Silence.

"The staff member said that I could stay with your family for a few days."

Silence.

"Hello-o-o-o!" I say loudly as I got a bit nervous.

"Hello! This is Kinko Ito. Can you hear me?"

For a moment, I am afraid that Mr. Kawanano might not understand my Japanese. *I have been living in the United States for over 32 years, but my Japanese cannot have deteriorated so badly that he cannot understand me.* I try to think rationally.

"*Ahhh*... I heard about you from the museum. As I have gotten older, I have become a bit hard of hearing, so please speak louder," Mr. Kawanano says finally.

"O-K-A-Y!!" I say slowly and distinctively. *Yokatta!* I feel relieved.

Later, Mr. Kawanano explained to me that he was outside of the house at the beginning of our conversation. There was a lot of noise, and it was difficult for him to hear me clearly.

Talking about hearing problems, my paternal grandfather also became hard of hearing in his 90s. He was a very healthy man who got up with the sun, worked hard in the fields, and enjoyed smoking cigarettes and eating Japanese sweets. He loved hot springs and traveling, too. I used to have tea and sweets with him and my mother until I left for the United States to pursue my graduate degrees.

My grandfather used to visit us at least once a week or so to bring the vegetables and grains he grew, or food cooked by his wife to our house, which was only a ten minutes' walk. My mother, being a hard-working kindergarten principal, really appreciated that. One day when I was in high school, my grandfather brought us vegetables in season. I was the only one in the house at about 4:30 pm. I offered him tea and told him that my mother would be back from work by 5:30 pm.

"Grandpa, why don't you wait for Mom?" I said and he agreed. My mother used to give him pocket money for the vegetables without him telling his wife or son (my uncle), and he always loved the extra money which he could use as he liked.

My mother came home soon enough bringing two boxes of Japanese sweets called *omanjū*. She said someone gave her one box as a gift.

"Why don't you open it?" My mother asked my grandfather, who smiled.

There were ten pieces of his favorite *omanjū* inside the box, and my mother said, "Grandpa, you can eat as much as you like. We have so many sweets here today to share."

His eyes twinkled with joy, and he ate six of them at once!

"Can I have another cup of green tea?" Grandfather asked, and I added hot water to the teapot and poured it into his cup. The Japanese sweets and green tea go together very well. The same green tea can vary from sweet to bitter depending on the number of brewing passes. Usually, you can brew a few cups of tea with the same leaves. It is also a custom not to add any sugar or cream to green tea.

My mother and grandfather got along exceptionally well. She always talked clearly and loudly to him so that he could hear her well in his old age. She also wrote down Chinese letters for homonyms[130] when they got a bit confusing. He really appreciated my mother's efforts in communication since he did not like to wear his hearing aid.

---

[130] The Japanese language has many homonyms (words that sound the same but have different meanings). When homonyms are written in Chinese characters, they are much easier to understand. The Japanese writing system has two different sets of Japanese characters that are derived from Kanji (Chinese characters), Chinese characters, and also Roman letters.

So much for my Grandfather, his hearing, and *omanjūs* and back to my phone call to the Ainu man.

Mr. Kawanano said during our conversation on the phone that nowadays he uses a hearing aid. I introduced myself to him again and restated the purpose for my visit. He said that he could pick me up at Japan Railway's (JR) Tomikawa Station, which is the closest station to Biratori. He said that I could visit any time that was convenient to my schedule. I had made plans to go to the *Poroto Kotan* and its Ainu Ethnic Museum in Shiraoi first and then spend a night in Tomakomai before taking a train to Tomikawa to meet Mr. Kawanano. I had searched the Japanese Jorudan Norikae Information web site to check on the train schedule from Tomakomai to Tomikawa, so that I could give my arrival time to Mr. Kawanano. We agreed to meet at 9 a.m. at Tomikawa Station on May 3.

My trip in 2011 was my second visit to Hokkaido. My parents and I did a sightseeing tour of Sapporo, Ostara, Noboribetsu, and Hakodate in the summer of 2004, which was my very first time on the northern island. We enjoyed the cities and the beautiful natural scenery of the sprawling countryside, which is rather rare in metropolitan areas surrounding big cities such as Tokyo, Yokohama, Nagoya, Kyoto, and Osaka in Honshu. My family loved tasting the rich variety of food available in Hokkaido. Definitely, *everything* tasted very good whether it was seafood (crabs, fish, fish eggs, and shellfish), grains, vegetables, dairy, or meat. For example, the milk they produce in Hokkaido is very delicious, and to me, a person from Honshu, it actually tastes much richer and creamier than that produced elsewhere in Japan does. The soft-serve ice cream I ate actually reminded me of some I had in Copenhagen, Denmark, a country well known for its dairy farming. Our tour guide told us that the secret of tasty dairy products was in the grass! The farmers in Hokkaido start with the grass that their cows eat. They research different types of grasses in order to find the one that would be best suited for the cows. This in turn would lead to better tasting milk. No wonder, the special milk makes other dairy products such as yogurt, cheese, ice cream, butter, butter candy, and caramel taste so good in Hokkaido. I bet the grass was also the secret ingredient for the very delicious meats with great flavors as well. Hokkaido has just about everything that a tourist desires, and I was excited about another opportunity to visit there during my sabbatical.

Figure 27 Dairy cows in Hokkaido.

Figure 28 A Biratori beefsteak lunch set with salad, grilled vegetables, and miso soup. The Biratori beef tastes as good as other famous Japanese beef such as Kobe, Matsusaka, Omi, etc. (at least to me), and it melts in your mouth.

Figure 29 Water surrounds Hokkaido - the Pacific Ocean, the Sea of Japan, and the Sea of Okhotsk. Thus, fresh and tasty seafood is abundant. The bowl on the right has slices of salmon, yellow tail, and salmon eggs marinated in soy sauce on a bed of sushi rice with wasabi and a slice of lemon. To its left is a baked potato. Salmon used to be an Ainu staple before the Japanese government banned catching them in 1870.

Figure 30 Fresh crabs sold at Nijo Market in Sapporo.

I scheduled my trip back to Hokkaido to start at the beginning of May in 2011. I picked this month because I thought the weather in Hokkaido would not be too cold. The temperature warms up a lot, and it is the beginning of a very comfortable spring. I also wanted to avoid the busy seasons: Hokkaido would be crowded with tourists from Honshu and abroad in the summer time, and many skiers and snowboarders go there to enjoy its wonderful powder snow in winter. By the way, the latitude of Sapporo, the capitol of Hokkaido, is 43 N, which is very close to that of Milwaukee, WI. Interestingly, Sapporo and Milwaukee produce beers, and Munich, a city in Germany also known for its beer, is located near the same latitude at 48 N.

"Make sure you take your *winter* clothes to Hokkaido. It is still definitely cold over there," my mother said on the phone when I called her from the United States right before my trip. I packed my coat, sweaters, warm winter underwear, scarves, camera, notebooks, and whatever I could think of. I had purchased a huge suitcase on sale at T.J. Maxx, and put everything in it. *This suitcase is heavy. It really is heavy for me*, I thought. It weighed about 40 pounds.

(2) My Trip to the Ainu Country

I went back and forth between Japan and the United States during my sabbatical in 2011. I left for Japan on April 25 to spend some time with my parents in Nagoya before my trip to Hokkaido. On the evening of May 1, I left my parents' house for a hotel near the Chubu International Airport. The next day I got up at 5 a.m., had breakfast, and walked to the airport, which took several minutes. I was to take a fight to Sapporo at 7 a.m. Sky Mark Airlines offered the cheapest fare available at the time (21,600 yen round trip: about US$200). The fare was actually cheaper than that of Japan Railways. I was not quite sure about the service of the so-called LCC (low-cost carrier), but it was a comfortable flight.

I landed at the Shinchitose Airport at 8:45 a.m., got my luggage, went to the Japan Railways station in the airport, and purchased my ticket to Tomakomai. I went outside to the platform to wait for my 9:34 a.m. train. Cold wind was blowing, and I could see snow-capped mountains far away. *Mom was right. It is so cold up here. I am glad I have my cap, Turkish silk scarf, and a nice coat!*

I was happy when the train arrived. It was warm and nice inside. I changed trains at Minami Chitose Station, which is only one station away from Shinchitose. I enjoyed the scenic train ride that wound through industrial parks, small towns, and pastures. The houses along the railway looked different from those in Honshu. Many of them have chimneys but no air-conditioners, and the design of their steep roofs prevents snow accumulation during winter. My train was not crowded at all, and the local passengers were mostly high school students, who talked in groups, played video games, or texted by themselves. There were also several middle-aged and elderly men and women. I looked for some Ainu faces because I was very curious how they might appear today, but all of the passengers looked *Wajin* (non-Ainu ethnic majority Japanese).

I get out of the train at Tomakomai Station at 9:57 a.m. and go to Toyoko-Inn, which is within a stone's throw. It is a national hotel chain mostly run by women from the executives to the staff members. As soon as I enter the hotel, I see two clerks standing at the front desk.

"*Ohayō gozaimasu!* (Good morning!) Welcome to Tomakomai!" they say cheerfully.

"*Ohayō gozaimasu!* I have a reservation for tonight, and I want to go to Shiraoi right now. Can you stow away my suitcase?"

"Sure, we can take care of it," one of them says.

"Here is your ticket. You can give it to us when you check in later. Have a nice trip to Shiraoi," the other one says.

"Please take care," they say in unison.

"Thank you," I say and leave the hotel.

I walk back to the nearby Tomakomai station to take a train to Shiraoi. For the next 27 minutes, I enjoy the landscape passing at a rapid pace.

(3) A Visit to *Poroto Kotan* and its Ainu Ethnic Museum in Shiraoi

Figure 31 Japan Railway's (JR) Shiraoi Station (2011).

I arrive at Shiraoi Station and head for an open-air museum called *Poroto Kotan*, which is a 15 minutes' walk or a short ride by taxi. I decide to take a cab.

In the Ainu language, *poro* means "big," *to* "a lake," and *kotan* means "community." As its name suggests, it is located right next to Lake Poroto. A huge statue of *kotankorkur* (the Chief of the community), which stands 16 meters (@17.5 yards) high, welcomes the visitors at the entrance. He is dressed in traditional Ainu clothes and a headdress for religious ceremonies. He has a full beard and moustache, too. He does look like a Chief!

Figure 32 A statue of *kotankorkur* (Chief of the community) looms high at the entrance to *Poroto Kotan* (2011).

Poroto Kotan is open from 8:45 a.m. to 5 p.m. every day except between December 29 and January 5. It is a time when people celebrate New Year's in Japan. The compound consists of several buildings such as the Ainu Ethnic Museum, five *cise*s (traditional Ainu houses with thatched roofs), a botanical garden (with 60 kinds of plants that are essential to the Ainu life), *pu* (storehouse), a bear cage, and a restaurant called Museum Café *Rimse* where customers can enjoy various Ainu dishes and soft-serve ice cream. (*Rimse* means "dance" in Ainu.) The museum has a shop that sells books about the Ainu, goods made by them, and souvenir gifts.

A building called "the Front House," which is adjacent to the Ainu Ethnic Museum, has a theater with a stage and rows of wooden benches for 216 people. I sit in the front row. The staff members offer a show at every hour throughout the day for the tourists, student groups, and others. Dressed in traditional and unique Ainu clothes and headdresses, they perform popular Ainu dances such as the crane dance by the women and the bow and arrow dance by the men. They also sing songs, and a woman plays the *mukkuri*. It is an Ainu mouth harp made of a strip of bamboo with a string attached to it. Traditionally, the dancing and singing have been a part of the Ainu's religious rituals to communicate with their gods. I really enjoy their performance. This is my first time watching their dancing and singing in person. In 1984, The Japanese government recognized traditional Ainu dancing as *Jūyō Mukei Bunkazai*,[131] an important intangible folk cultural asset, and it gave the Ainu people pride and esteem.

Among the entries of the performances at *Poroto Kotan* is a trivia quiz show in which a male staff member who looks more *Wajin* asks several questions regarding the ethnic group.

"Hello! And welcome to *Poroto Kotan!*" The MC says to the audience with a big smile.

"I am going to ask you some questions now. Are you ready?"

"Yes!" Some people respond. It is a very lively audience.

"Okay. There are several delivery service companies in Japan, and the name of one of them derives from the Ainu language. Which company is it?"

"I know!" A young man says as he raises his hand.

The MC points at him, and he asks him, "Okay, what is it?"

"It's Kangaroo, isn't it?"

"Oh, I am sorry. Kangaroo is an Australian aboriginal word," the MC says.

"What about Pelican?" another man says.

"No, I am sorry. Pelican is an English word deriving from Greek which means an ax."

"*Kuroneko*," a young student says. (*Kuroneko* is a Japanese word that means "black cat.")

"No, it's not an Ainu word," the MC says.

I know the answer and raise my hand.

"*Ojōchan* (Little Miss) over there," the MC points at me.

I smile a bit but feel funny that he addresses me as a "Little Miss" since I am in my 50's! *His eyesight might not be good,* I think. *Ojōchan* is too much of a compliment for a woman of my age, but I must confess that many people have complimented me on my beautiful complexion I inherited genetically.

"What is the answer?" The MC asks.

"*Tonakai!*" I answer with confidence.

"Little Miss, you are correct! The Ainu word does mean 'reindeer' in Japanese! You are so smart!" The MC says with a big smile. I feel a bit awkward about his compliment, but what the heck, I studied a lot about the Ainu before I came to this museum.

---

[131] www.city.chitose.lg.jp/docs/95-3261-169-915.html. Accessed 2/3/2019.

"OK, now. What is the name of a famous and popular Japanese magazine whose name derives from the Ainu language?" He asks the audience again.

"Magazine!"

"Sunday!"

"Jump!"

Several young men list names of very popular boys' comic magazines.

"Orange Page!" A woman gives the name of a popular Japanese women's journal.

These are definitely English words! The audience must not have studied English seriously when they were in high school, I think.

I raise my hand again and with confidence.

"Okay, you again." The MC points at me.

I smile and say "*Nonno!*"

"You are right again! Do you know its meaning by any chance?"

"Yes, I do. It means a flower," I say. The MC seems to be quite impressed.

"Next, this is the last question. What is the name of an animal that is comical and very popular in Japan? You can find them in the zoos, and they look very cute floating in water with their babies on their stomachs."

Several people name different kinds of animals, but they are all wrong. I raise my hand again.

"*Ojōchan*, please answer," the MC says,

"It is *rakko* (a sea otter)."

"*Ojō-chan*, you know a lot about the Ainu. Where are you from?" The MC asks me with curiosity.

"America," I answer. He raises his eyebrows and says, "Oh!"

"What do you do over there? Are you a student?"

"No, I am a professor of sociology," I say.

The MC seems to be embarrassed to death, and the audience feels sorry for him. It was a very good quiz show though. He thanks me for coming all the way from the United States to Shiraoi to participate, and I say "*Iyairaikere* (Thank you)" with a smile.

I read about a dozen books on the Ainu by the time I went to Shiraoi's *Poroto Kotan* during my sabbatical. Thus, I was definitely more informed than the general audience who were tourists there. After the show, the MC and I talked right outside of the small theater. He seemed to be interested in me, and I informed him that I am doing research on the Ainu. I also complimented him on his show and told him that I really enjoyed all the performances. He wished me luck when we said good-bye.

It is now time for lunch, and I walk to the nearby Museum Café Rimse. The outside temperature is 7 C (45 F), and it feels like winter even though it is May.

BRRRRRRRRRRRRRRRRRRR. It is so chilly here. I am very happy I listened to my mother's advice and have the appropriate outerwear.

"Hello! May I help you?" A woman at the counter says to me smiling. I look up the menu and decide to try *ohaw*, which is a traditional Ainu soup dish.

"It will be ready soon," she tells me with a smile. I am so hungry I cannot wait!

"Please sit wherever you want. I will bring it to your table."

"Thank you," I say to her politely, and she soon shows up with my order.

Figure 33 My lunch special at Café Rimse in *Poroto Kotan*: salmon *ohaw*, inakibi rice, daikon radish pickles, and herb tea.

Wow! This is my very first Ainu meal! I am really excited and eager to try it. Inside the huge bowl are pieces of salmon, potato, *daikon* radish, carrots, and green onions. The smell is very enticing, and the hot soup is really inviting in this cold weather. Interestingly, the only seasoning for the soup is salt. It definitely is a simple yet very delicious dish. *The great soil of Hokkaido produces these great tasting veggies*, I think as I enjoy eating the soup that had been warming my body. There are very small grains of yellow *inakibi* in my rice, and thus they call the dish *inakibi* rice. I find it very tasty and like *inakibi* beads popping in my mouth. My lunch costs me only 500 yen, less than US$5. It is a steal!

After lunch, I visit each *cise* (traditional Ainu house) which has different exhibits and cultural activities that tourists can try for a nominal fee. Tourists can watch the women staff members weave and sew clothes and teach the tourists how to make and play the *mukkuri* (a mouth harp). There are also classes offered on how to embroider and sculpture with Ainu designs.

Figure 34 The Entrance to the Ainu Ethnic Museum in *Poroto Kotan* (2011).

In the main building of the museum, I had a chance to talk with one of the female staff members. A man who works for one of the museums in Biratori happened to know her, and he kindly arranged my meeting with her in *Poroto Kotan*. I went to the receptionist, asked for her, and waited for a few minutes. She seemed to know who I was when she came to see me. She invited me to a room where we could talk in private. We sat down at a table.

"My name is Kinko Ito, as you already know. Here is my business card," I hand her my card with both hands and bow.

"Here is mine," she gives me hers with a bow.

"I have been on my sabbatical this semester and studying about the Ainu people, mainly reading books on them. I would really appreciate it if you can tell me anything about them," I say.

"There are pros and cons about being an Ainu, and that is why some Ainu people who can pass as *Wajin* (non-Ainu ethnic majority Japanese) might not want to come out and publicly say that they are Ainu," she says.

"I see," I nod.

"I am an Ainu," she says.

"You are?" I say.

"Yes," she responds with a smile.

"You can pass as a pretty *Wajin* woman. You might look a bit exotic, but it is a positive exotic, you know," I say to her honestly.

"Thank you," the staff member smiles. She continues, "My father is a *Wajin* and my mother is an Ainu. We do not speak Ainu at home or anywhere. We are in an environment in which we cannot speak the language comfortably anyway. The language needs new vocabulary that matches the needs of contemporary people who use technology and have new concepts that our ancestors did not have."

"Did you experience any negative things at school while you were growing up?" I ask.

"Yes. Kids can be very cruel. For example, when I would go to school, some *Wajin* boys used to ridicule me saying '*Ainu ga kita*,' a typical insult to an Ainu person," she says. (*Ainu ga kita* can be divided to *A inu ga kita*, which literally means "Ah *inu* (dog) is coming!")

"I see," I comment and feel badly about the verbal abuse.

She says, "This is just a beginning. The kids would say so many bad things that would hurt the feelings of the Ainu people. I am not going to repeat them to you. Anyway, I myself have understood and felt that the word Ainu itself is a derogatory and discriminating term. People would say, 'She does such and such because she is an Ainu' Or, 'She wants to do this and that when she is only an Ainu.' If you have any Ainu blood, they brand you as an Ainu and treat you accordingly," she adds.

"What has been the best thing that happened to you as an Ainu?" I am curious.

"I was hired by this museum because I am an Ainu," she smiled. "An Ainu person has advantages because this museum is about the Ainu, their culture, history, everyday life, etc. More than half the employees have Ainu blood.

"The Ainu Culture Promotion Law in 1997 and the Japanese government's recognition that we are the indigenous people in 2008 have helped us regarding our cultural activities. However, other things remain just about the same as before. Many Ainu themselves do not know their own history of exploitation and oppression. Discrimination and reverse discrimination have been taking place. For example, the Ainu feels discriminated against when someone says 'Play with that girl because she is an Ainu' or 'Don't play with her because she is an Ainu.' It hurts either way.

"I love my parents, but I associated the word Ainu with negative images. Many Ainu do not do so in the last few years and feel comfortable using the word. Our family registration paper does not say that we are of Ainu origin, and it is up to an individual whether she identifies herself with the Ainu or not. For me, I did not like being an Ainu. I felt inferior. I hated other kids bullying me at school, and I pitied myself. However, my siblings view the Ainu in a more positive way even though we are from the same family. I am wondering about what makes an Ainu, and I still ask myself who I am," she adds.

"What should the government do to eliminate this kind of problem?" I ask her.

"I think education is very important. Both the *Wajin* and Ainu should learn about the history of Hokkaido. Public assistance and scholarships would help the Ainu in order to focus and get involved with cultural activities. Economic stability is must for them to keep their traditions. I hope I answered your questions satisfactorily," she says.

"Thank you so much for your time," I say and smile to her.

"You are welcome and good luck with your research," she says and sees me off as leave the room. I move to the exhibition area. A male volunteer, who is a retired schoolteacher, offers me a tour of the museum. He kindly explains just about every single exhibit.

I am especially interested in the food exhibit. The volunteer staff member says to me in front of the fishing exhibit, "Salmon is very important not only as a food source but it is also used in the Ainu rituals. The fish were abundant everywhere in Hokkaido in those days. Starting in 1870, the new Meiji government prohibited the Ainu from fishing salmon in rivers. Salmon had been the native people's staple food. However, when they 'poach' salmon in their backyard, they become criminals, and they go to a prison. Telling them not to fish salmon meant 'Death to the Ainu,'" he says with tears welling up in his eyes. I am very touched by this, and I get emotional, too. The salmon soup I had for lunch was so delicious that my heart aches.

My guide keeps talking as I keep looking at the arrow and trap exhibits, "The Meiji government also prohibited the Ainu from using their traditional poisonous arrows and spring-loaded poison traps in 1876. The poison is derived from *aconite* (a wild flower), and each Ainu family possessed a recipe that was carefully guarded.

"Hunting deer was barred in 1889. In the 1880s, the Ainu suffered from many famines. The Ainu's basic rights to live in their own homeland vanished, and the population fell due to poverty and starvation. Many new immigrants from Honshu (mainland) brought tuberculosis, sexually transmitted diseases, and measles, which had not previously existed in Hokkaido."

All of these prohibitions and the spread of new diseases definitely contributed to ethnic cleansing, and I also thought that the Ainu suffered from what Göran Therborn terms *vital inequality*, which is "inequality of life and death – that is, of differential exposure to fatal risk."[132] Vital inequality is measured by life expectancy, mortality and morbidity rates, health, and malnutrition.

According to the staff member, what the Meiji Government did in Hokkaido in the name of "development" was nothing but plunder, exploitation, and oppression of the Ainu. The Colonization Board exposed the Ainu to unfair, unbearable, and unjustifiable hardships in their homeland just like many other indigenous groups of the world.

This historical movement has something to do with what was going on politically in the region. Several super powers including Russia were interested in Hokkaido, and the Japanese government decided to assimilate the Ainu. The Japanese government forced the Ainu to become Japanese citizens and eliminate their unique cultural traditions and language.

The museum also has exhibits on Ainu crafts such as hand-sewn clothes made of tree bark with intricate embroidery, everyday tools for hunting, fishing, and cooking, items for religious rituals, textiles, ceremonial clothes and head dress, etc. A visitor can learn about the history of colonial development in Hokkaido and the Ainu. I spent the total of six hours at the

---

[132] Göran Therborn. 2006, p.6.

museum, and I left when it was closing at 5 p.m. My visit to *Poroto Kotan* was not only educational but also entertaining. Time went very fast. I had a lot of fun looking at the artifacts and learned a lot about the Ainu's history, life style, and material and non-material culture. No wonder there were many groups of students who were visiting it on a school excursion as well as tourists from abroad.

On March 31, 2018, *Poroto Kotan* closed its doors permanently after so many decades of successful operation for educating the public about the Ainu. The whole area will become the National Ainu Ethnic Museum and Park. They will open on April 24, 2020[133]. It will serve as a national center for reviving, creating, and promoting Ainu culture as well as a place where people can learn about the history, tradition, and culture of the Ainu.[134]

---

[133] www.ainu-museum.or.jp/kokuritsu/pdf/2020_kokuritsu03.pdf. Accessed 2/24/19.

[134] www.ainu-upopoy.jp. Accessed 2/3/2019.

Chapter 5: My First Homestay at the Kawananos (2011)

On May 3, I got up at 6:30 a.m. and had free breakfast at my hotel. The breakfast was a buffet, and the guests could enjoy both Japanese breakfast (rice, *onigiri* rice balls, miso soup, pickles, eggs, green tea, etc.) and/or western breakfast (toast, bread, jam, butter, coffee, etc.). I had been eating breakfast by myself for a while when a woman said to me, "Do you mind if I share the table?"

"No, not at all. Please join me," I said to the middle-aged woman. Her name was Hiroko, and she said she was from Saitama. She told me that she loves Hokkaido, and she was on a trip during the Golden Week.[135] She showed a lot of interest in my life in the United States, and we had a great time talking over breakfast. Hiroko was so friendly and nice that it did not really feel like our first meeting.

I checked out of the hotel and took the 8:03 a.m. train from Tomakomai to Tomikawa, where Mr. Kawanano would pick me up at 9:00 a.m. I was excited about my trip. At the beginning of the train ride, there were so many people that I could not find a seat. I had a black leather backpack and a huge light-blue suitcase whose size was rare in Japan where people travel lightly. I stood in the space between the two cars and decided to wait until enough people got out of the train at the next station.

"Excuse me, but where are you going?" A decent looking, middle-aged woman, a total stranger who seemed several years older than I, asks me politely.

"I am going to Tomikawa," I reply wondering why she is interested in me.

"*Ahh, so*. Do you have friends there?"

"No, but someone is waiting for me at the station to take me to Biratori," I answer.

"You are going to Biratori?"

"Yes."

"You have such a huge suitcase, don't you? How long are you traveling?" she says inspecting my suitcase closely.

What is wrong with this woman asking me such questions as if I am a criminal when I am just another passenger on the train?

"About ten days. I came all the way from America. I am a professor of sociology and am going to do research there," I say.

"Oh, I see. I am very sorry to have bothered you." *Okay, she is sorry now*, I think.

"It's okay," I say to her.

"I am a social worker, and I thought you were running away from your abusive husband or a debt collector, or something like that. You are going to do research. That's nice. Good luck," she says and exits the train at the next station.

Some Japanese people seem to be concerned about and react to a person with a huge suitcase. With the emergence of all kinds of terrorism worldwide today, the suitcase might raise suspicion. Maybe… However, I remember being stopped by a police officer on a street in Tokyo in the late 1980s and was asked to come to a mini police station nearby. He said he wanted to ask me some questions related to his job. I was then wearing a thick purple winter coat over my

---

[135] A Golden Week takes place from the end of April to the beginning of May when several national holidays and a weekend make a long "vacation" time for the busy Japanese. It starts with April 29th, which used to be the national holiday for Emperor Hirohito's birthday and now is called Showa Day, May 3rd (Constitution Memorial Day) and May 4th (Greenery Day) followed by May 5th, the Children's Day.

green sweatshirt and pants and carrying a large suitcase with wheels. I had just arrived from the U.S. and wanted to visit my friend in Tokyo before I went to Nagoya to spend my Christmas break with my family. I was a graduate student in Ohio, and I admit that I was dressed rather poorly. The police officer let me go after I showed him my student ID and passport.

I told this incident to my parents when I arrived at home. My mother said that possibly the police officer thought I was a prostitute or a runaway teenager, or some kind of a criminal or, maybe a person who is socially unfit. *Now, some thirty years later when I am a professor, this woman on the train still thinks that I somehow was running away!*

I kept standing for a while and found an empty seat at the next station. It was more comfortable sitting on a seat and looking out of the window instead of standing and hanging onto my big suitcase and carry-on at the same time. The distance between the stations seemed much longer than that in Honshu. In metropolitan areas, it usually takes an average of two to four minutes between the stations while in Hokkaido it was several minutes, and occasionally longer.

Figure 35 From Japan Railway's (JR) Yufutsu Station you can see a paper mill.

Figure 36 Hokkaido does look wild, doesn't it?

Figure 37 Enormous pile of coal (?) seen from my train window.

Figure 38 The Pacific Ocean.

My train passed through scenic places – I could see the ocean, pastures, factories, shops and houses from the window, and it was fun riding it. I thought of my grandparents who traveled with my father to Hokkaido in July 1962. In spite of the fact that my mother was pregnant with my brother, and her due date was coming up very soon, my father escorted his parents for a weeklong vacation. They visited their relatives, friends, and a man who boarded in my grandparents' house for a few years back in the 1950s when he was working in Nagoya. As I looked out of the window of my train, I wondered what it was like to travel by rail in Hokkaido in those days.

I was anxious about meeting Mr. Kawanano. *What does he look like?* I wondered and looked at the passengers in the car. I could not tell who was an Ainu and who was not. As my train was approaching my destination, I went to the very front of the train, stood right behind the driver, and looked out of the window.

Figure 39 The view from the front of the train.

At Tomikawa Station, I was one of the very few passengers who got off the train. An old man was waiting in his van in front of the station. *He must be Mr. Kawanano*, I instinctively thought. He was just about the only one who seemed to be waiting. I had been quite excited as I approached his van before he got out of the vehicle. He waved at me.

"Hello!" Mr. Kawanano says.

"Are you Mr. Kawanano?" I ask politely just to make sure he is the right man.

"Yes," he says with a smile.

To my surprise, Mr. Kawanano's facial features reminded me of my grandfather who passed away in the 1980s. It was funny that I had been thinking about my grandparents as I rode the train today. I am not sure if I am a psychic or not, but when I think of something, that very something sometimes happens or appears. For example, when I am thinking of a friend, I sometimes get a call from him or her in a few minutes. When I called a professor in Japan, he answered and said, "Guess what I have in my hand right now. I have my address book with me because I was going to call you!" Likewise I sometimes get e-mails and other forms of correspondence (letters, cards, gifts, etc.) when I think of someone. Anyway, it had been a while since I last saw my Grandpa alive, and thus I was very happy to meet Mr. Kawanano.

"I am Kinko Ito. It is very nice to meet you. Thank you so much for taking time to pick me up," I say to him.

"No problem! Let me help you with your luggage," he says and puts my large suitcase in the back of his van.

"It's heavy, isn't it?" I say. "I am sorry to bother you with it."

"It's okay. Now we are ready to go!" he says as he shuts the door of his van.

"Yes, let's," I say.

"Are you wearing your seatbelt?" he asks me.

"Yes!"

It was exciting for me to ride with Mr. Kawanano, who used to go to Honshu during winter months to work as a truck driver. Mr. Kawanano drove me to various places in town as he talked about the Ainu people and himself. At one point, I was surprised to see a sign written in red letters that said, "Watch out for bears – Biratori Town." Mr. Kawanano said that bears do appear and attack humans in Hokkaido!

"Do they really attack them!?" I ask him.

"They sure do, and we must be careful," Mr. Kawanano says as if it is not really a big deal.

Figure 40 This sign near a bridge bears a warning "Watch out for bears – Biratori Town."

Mr. Kawanano drove me to a plaza in Nibutani where several traditional Ainu buildings (houses, storehouses, a bear cage, etc.) and boats curved out of tree trunks are exhibited in open air with information boards for tourists and for educational purposes. There are huge parking lots nearby for the tourist buses and visitors' cars.

Figure 41 Several tourist buses parked in a huge parking lot in Nibutani (2012).

Figure 42 A device for using waterpower to mill rice. Water goes into the container on the right side and the pounder on the left pounds the rice. There were about 40 of these in Nibutani, which had about 50 Ainu households between 1935 and 1945.

Figure 43 A traditional Ainu boat made from a tree bears carved Ainu designs (2012).

Mr. Kawanano and I get out of his van and go into one of the showcase *cises*. We open the door and stand in the entrance hall.

"Hello!" Mr. Kawanano says loudly and happily, to an old woman who is sitting on a chair making threads and listening to a cassette tape in Ainu language.

"Oh! *Irankarapte!* (Hello!)" The woman says and looks up from her work.

"How are you?" Mr. Kawanano asks her.

"Fine, fine," she responds with a smile. I can tell that they have known each other for a long time and are very good friends from the way they interact.

"How about you?" she says to Mr. Kawanano.

Figure 44 Mrs. Sachiko (Satchan) Kibata. She is wearing a *rektunpe* around her neck. She is very friendly and has a great sense of humor. She helped me with my interviews in 2012 and with videotaping for my documentary film in 2014.

"I'm fine, thank you. Let me introduce this woman from America," Mr. Kawanano says.

"Her name is Kinko Ito, and she has a doctorate degree. She teaches sociology at a university and wants to learn about the Ainu," he says proudly.

"Nice to meet you," I bow to her and hand her my business card with both hands.

"This is Satchan, I mean, Mrs. Sachiko Kibata. She is also an Ainu," Mr. Kawanano says.

"Come in! Come in! Let's have some tea and talk," friendly Satchan says waving her hand with the palm facing downward. Her smile is welcoming to us.

We remove our shoes, put them away nicely, and step up to the floor where there are special handmade mats. It is customary in Japan to take one's shoes off in the entrance hall before entering the house space. In the Shinto tradition, people do not want to bring any defilement of the outside world into their sacred home. (Shinto is an indigenous, animistic, and polytheistic religion of Japan. Interestingly, when I visited my Muslim friends' homes in Turkey, they asked me to take off my shoes, too!)

I follow Mr. Kawanano who goes to sit by the fire pit in the middle of the *cise*.

"Please use these cushions," Satchan offers us cushions to sit on.

"*Iyairaikere* (Thank you)," I say.

"Oh, you speak Ainu!?" she says smiling. She seems delighted and pleasantly surprised by my Ainu greetings.

"No, I only know a few words," I say humbly.

"I want to learn more about the language though," I add.

Satchan has been playing her cassette tape recorder as she works on making threads, and I ask her, "I'm sorry, but what are you listening to?"

"*Ahh*, this. I am listening to stories in Ainu. As you might already know, the Ainu language does not have written words, so everything was transmitted orally," she explains.

"I see," I say.

"I need to listen to these tapes and keep up my Ainu language. I am an instructor at the Ainu language school in town," she says.

Mr. Kawanano checks the burning wood in the fire pit.

"Fire is considered sacred by the Ainu, and we give prayers and offerings to *Apefuci Kamuy*, 'the Goddess of Fire'," he explains to me.

Figure 45 Gods are everywhere in the Ainu religion. The Goddess of Fire is one of the most important, and the Ainu pray to her first and then pray to other gods.

"The fire inside the *cise* sometimes caused the air to be very smoky. Many Ainu people used to suffer from bad eyes and diseases due to the smoke," Mr. Kawanano says.

"Please have some tea and sweets," Satchan brings them to us.

Mr. Kawanano and Satchan engage in catching up with each other and report on other Ainu people, and they truly seem to be happy together. Satchan keeps working on making thread out of tree fiber as she talks with him. She says that she uses the thread to make traditional mats that are placed on the floor in a *cise*.

Figure 46 Satchan is making a cord as she talks with Mr. Kawanano.

Figure 47 Threads made from all natural materials – tree fiber.

Figure 28 A close up of Satchan's hands making a cord.

Figure 49 Satchan uses these threads for weaving traditional mats.

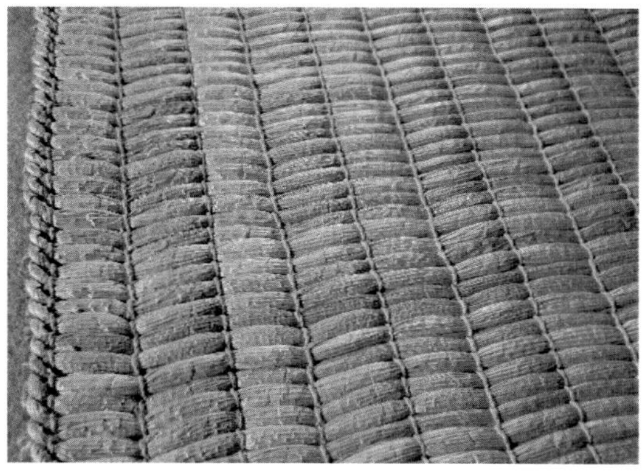

Figure 50 A traditional mat made of tree fiber.

"What was it like growing up Ainu?" I ask Satchan. I might as well get some information about their lives while we have time together.

"When I was young I was bullied and ridiculed by *Wajin* kids. When I went home from school, they would call me repeatedly '*Kotan biiru* (kotan beer)! *Kotan biiru!*' because there were many Ainu drunkards walking around smelling like alcohol in town in those days. *Kotan* is an Ainu word that means 'a community.' My father worked, made money, and spent it all on drinking. We were poor, and it was difficult," Satchan says.

"My friend Tome-san once said laughing, 'When a tiger dies, it leaves its leather. When an Ainu dies, he leaves a whole bunch of liquor bottles behind' Alcohol was a problem for many Ainu men in those days," Mr. Kawanano added.

"I've heard about Native Americans' drinking problems in the reservations and other places, but I did not know that the Ainu had the same problem," I make a comment.

"I assume that many of them just had to drink alcohol in order to forget about their hardships. *Wajin* liquor owners took advantage of their drunkenness, and they cheated on them when they purchased liquor on credit. If the Ainu could not pay the bill, certain *Wajin* storeowners demanded that the Ainu pay the bill with land. That is how they started to own more and more land, and the poor Ainu got poorer," Mr. Kawanano says.

"I see," I say.

"Well, I am glad you could meet Satchan today. Shall we keep going?" Mr. Kawanano says to me after a while.

"Sure," I respond.

"Satchan, thank you for your hospitality. We need to visit the museums now," Mr. Kawanano says.

"*Iyairaikere* (Thank you)!" I say to Satchan.

"*Iyairaikere.* It was very nice of you stop by here. Come back again any time, okay?" she says.

"*Jā* (See you)," Mr. Kawanano says waving his hand to her.

"*Sayonara!* (Good-bye)" Satchan says to me.

"*Sayonara!* Thank you!" I thank her again and leave the *cise*.

Mr. Kawanano and I leave the *cise* and walk to Nibutani Ainu Cultural Museum, which takes only a few minutes. We visit a staff member, who sent me an e-mail and arranged my stay with the Kawananos. He invited us in, and introduced me to another young and handsome staff member. He happily offered me drinks.

Figure 51 Mr. Kawanano in front of the Nibutani Ainu Cultural Museum, with its very modern architecture (2011).

"Dr. Kinko, what would you like to drink? Green tea? Coffee?" the handsome young staff member says with a smile.

"Thank you, but I would like to have hot water," I say politely.

"Hot water?"

"Yes, hot water. I would like to have it *chinchin*, if you could make it that way," I say politely.

The young man blushes.

"What!?" he seems to be thinking.

The other staff member laughs and explains that *chinchin* means "extremely hot" in my dialect.

"I see," he says looking still a bit embarrassed.

"Oh, I am sorry! I did not mean to embarrass you," I apologize.

"Around Aichi and Gifu prefectures in the central part of Japan, the local people almost always use the term for scalding hot temperature of liquids such as drinking water or bath water," I explain to him.

Chinchin is one of the words that refers to a penis in Japanese. The Japanese affectionately call it *ochinchin*. The prefix *o* makes the word that follows it more polite, honorable, and respectful when speaking to another person. The examples include *o-namae* (name), *o-biiru* (beer), and *okanjō* (bill). In my case, I used *chinchin* as an adverb instead of a noun. The young man thought it was a noun and misunderstood the "naughty" middle-aged woman from America. There was no intended sexual harassment on my part. Mr. Kawanano, the two staff members, and I all laugh so hard. We have a nice talk together as we drink and eat sweets in the office for a while.

Mr. Kawanano and I say "Thank you" to the young staff members, leave the staff room, and move to the exhibit areas of the museum. I looked at the cooking utensils, traditional clothing, farming equipment, and other items used in the Ainu everyday life. I notice that Mr. Kawanano becomes a bit emotional when he talks about certain memories of the items. He might be feeling nostalgic about his past or family.

In late afternoon, Mr. Kawanano says he will take me to his house in Nioi, where many Ainu people reside. The mountains and the river near their house are simply beautiful.

Figure 52 A beautiful view of the fogged-in mountains from the residence of the Kawananos.

"Here we are. This is my house," Mr. Kawanano says and stops the engine of his van.

"It's a modern house," I say.

It is my first time visiting a private home in Hokkaido, and I notice that there is a small room with glass doors at the entrance. I can see snow boots on the floor and winter coats on the rack. There is another door before you enter the house. Obviously, this is to deal with the cold and long winter of Hokkaido. I take off my shoes after Mr. Kawanano and enter the house.

"Welcome," his wife comes out of the room next to the entrance and greets us.

"This is Motoko," Mr. Kawanano says.

"Hello! Nice to meet you," I say.

"Nice to meet you," his wife says. She seems to be a very friendly person.

"Come in, and let's have tea," she suggests.

Mr. Kawanano tells Motoko what we have been doing in town since he picked me up at the Tomikawa Station this morning. I eat the sweets and drink green tea, and interestingly enough, I feel right at home.

The temperature is dropping in the evening, and the Kawananos put firewood to their stove. Many readers (Yes, you!) might believe that Japan has a temperate climate thanks to its size, which is about the size of Montana in the United States. This statement is mostly true.

However, Japan is a country shaped like a crescent in East Asia. The nation extends 3,000 km (1,860 miles) from tip to tip[136], which is equivalent to the distance between Montreal,

136 Nippon Steel Corporation Personnel Development Division. 1984, pp.31-33.

Canada to Kingston, Jamaica (1,924 miles). Thus, the temperature varies widely. When my friend Kay and I visited Okinawa in May 2007, we went to the beach to walk along. We also swam in the warm water where we found tropical fish normally seen in pet shops! Here in Hokkaido, it is also May, but the Kawananos are burning firewood!

Figure 53 The Kawananos are putting firewood into the stove placed at the center of the living room.

The stove has a chimney, and it is in the middle of the carpeted living room. They place kettles on top of the stove so that they function as humidifiers. They use the hot water for cooking, drinking, and laundry.

The next day, Mr. Kawanano takes me to the home of Mrs. Reiko Kayano, the widow of Shigeru Kayano and the mother of Shiro Kayano. She lives in a modern house with a huge living room with nice furniture. I see a few calendars on the walls. She welcomes us with the most delicious green tea and steamed potatoes. She suggests for me to add salt and butter. They are divine! I ask Reiko-san some questions about her life, to which she happily replies. Mr. Kawanano and Reiko-san later sing Ainu ballads and songs together for me. I am very flattered. It is simply so beautiful that it makes me feel nostalgic and emotional as well.

Figure 54 Reiko-san's most delicious potatoes and a box of Yotsuba Butter.

Mr. Kawanano and I thank Reiko-san for her hospitality and leave her house to go to the Historical Museum of the Saru River, which is located right next to Nibutani Ainu Cultural Museum. He happily has become my main informant and liaison, and he proudly introduces me to the welcoming and friendly staff members at the museum as if I am his own daughter. I feel very happy and honored. They also introduce me to many Ainu people in town, both Ainu and *Wajin* (non-Ainu majority ethnic Japanese).

In all, I learned a lot about the Ainu culture during my short stay with Mr. and Mrs. Kawanano in 2011: visits to museums where the knowledgeable staff members explained archaeological history, Ainu art, and folk artifacts and talking with their friends. At their home, I ate traditional Ainu food such as *ohaw* (soup with salmon and vegetables in a slightly salted broth) and *inakibi* rice (rice with barnyard millet) in addition to regular Japanese meals. Mr. Kawanano and his wife Motoko showed me proudly several beautiful, hand-sewn, traditional Ainu clothing pieces, a handmade ceremonial crown, bandanas with embroidery, and hand-woven *saranip* handbags. It was their "show and tell" time, and it was quite entertaining for me. They wore these items themselves just like models. To my surprise, they let me wear them, and take pictures, as well. *Welcome to the Wonderful World of the Ainu!* I really enjoyed my stay with the Kawananos.

Figure 55 Mr. and Mrs. Kawanano are dressed in traditional Ainu clothing, a religious headdress, and a bandana with Ainu design embroidery.

The next day, Motoko showed me how to make and embroider a traditional wardrobe with *Attus* cloth, which is made of *ohyō* (Japanese elm tree). Motoko said that it takes up to three years to make a complete garment. Mr. Kawanano explained that *ohyō*'s fibers from the barks are strong, make long threads easily, and are hand-woven into cloth. The cloth is bulky yet soft enough to wear as a garment. Motoko sews pieces of cloth onto *Attus* and embroiders various Ainu designs to make a traditional wardrobe for the religious and other ceremonies.

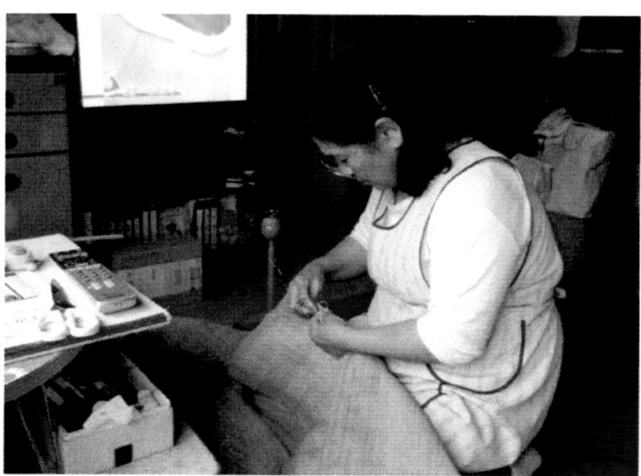

Figure 56 Motoko is making an *Attus* gown for her husband.

Figure 57 The back of an *attus* gown with beautiful cotton appliques and intricate Ainu design embroidery.

The time came too soon for me to say good-bye to my Ainu hosts. Before I left their house for a long distance bus stop on May 4, 2011, Mr. Kawanano said to me, "Like many other Ainu elders, I am not young anymore, and my years are limited. I am very happy that you are studying the Ainu. You know English and Spanish, and you can reach out to more people and let them know about us. I really appreciate that. Please come back next year. I will introduce you to more Ainu people. This is your home, and you are welcome here any time. I will be waiting for you."

My next destination was Sapporo, the capital and the largest city in Hokkaido. I said thank you and good-bye to Motoko, and Mr. Kawanano drove me to a bus stop in Tomikawa. I was to take a long distance express bus called Pegasus at 4:10 pm. We arrived at the stop early, and we had more time to talk. I was very happy that I decided to visit Biratori-cho and met the Kawananos and other Ainu and *Wajin* people. Time passed by, and I know I was getting very emotional as my departure got near. I met Mr. Kawanano only yesterday, but it felt like I had known him for a long time. Maybe it was because he resembled my deceased grandfather. Maybe it was because the Ainu have been known for their hospitality and kindness. Maybe… Maybe I started to have an attachment to this place…

"Well, take care, and come back. I will be waiting," Mr. Kawanano said as my bus showed up on the street.

"Thank you so much for everything. I really enjoyed staying with you and meeting your friends. I will find a way to come back next year," I said to him cheerfully.

I waved my hand to him from the bus window, and he waved back. I saw his car leave the parking lot. Tears started to well up in my eyes. I knew I was not crying because I was sad, but because I was impressed with the kindness and warmth of the Kawananos and others whom I met in Biratori. They accepted me with their open hands and took care of me so well. As mentioned before, the Ainu greeting *Irankarapte* literally means "Let me gently touch your heart," and my heart was truly touched.

My express bus arrived at Sapporo Station at 5:50 pm. I could see my friend Rieko and her husband waiting for me at the bus stop. Rieko was an elementary school teacher in Sapporo when she did school visits in Little Rock, Arkansas in the middle of 1990s. She later became a vice principal and a principal before she retired. We became very good friends, and Rieko came to stay at my parents' house in Nagoya a few times. She had been insisting that I visit her and her husband in Sapporo.

On May 5, 2011, I visited Hokkaido Museum and the adjacent Historical Village of Hokkaido. On May 6, I visited Hokkaido Ainu Minzoku Bunka Kenkyū Center and Ainu Sōgō Center. The staff members at these places were very friendly and helpful: they welcomed me and answered all my questions. I did some sightseeing with Rieko on the weekend and went back to my parents' house on the ninth. Overall, it was a very educational and productive trip for me.

Figure 58 Hokkaido Museum in Sapporo. I highly recommend a visit to this museum for anyone who is interested in the Ainu.

Figure 59 A museum staff member is reconstructing pottery with the broken pieces from ancient times.

Figure 60 At Historical Village of Hokkaido, an open-air museum with important buildings from Hokkaido's past.

Figure 61 The Hokkaido Colonial Board building (1871) at Historical Village of Hokkaido.

Figure 62 A western building from the Meiji period at Historical Village of Hokkaido. It used to be in Urakawa.

Chapter 6: The Story of Mr. Kazunobu Kawanano: My Ainu "Father"[137]

Mr. Kazunobu Kawanano was born in what is today's Biratori Town in 1934. His grandmother became a widow when Kazunobu was very young, and she came to live with his family until he finished elementary school. She spoke the Ainu language with her friends in the community, with whom she would occasionally get together and enjoy story telling all night. That is how Kazunobu came to understand some Ainu language. However, his parents, just like many other Ainu parents in those days, encouraged him to speak only Japanese. Kazunobu said to me. "I did not have to learn the Ainu language because my parents spoke Japanese at home. They did not think I needed to speak it even though I was surrounded by older people who spoke Ainu all the time."[138]

Many Ainu parents themselves thought that speaking Japanese would promote assimilation and prevent prejudice, discrimination, and bullying at school. According to Kazunobu, "The Ainu had been looked down upon and discriminated against in society throughout the Meiji and Taisho Periods (1868 to 1926), and the Ainu elders thought that their children should study Japanese only. Thus, they spoke the Ainu language among themselves, but they only spoke Japanese to us children." The Ainu had been encouraged to learn and speak Japanese by the government starting in 1871, which was part of the forced assimilation policy.

Kazunobu continued, "I am sorry that I am not a native speaker of Ainu. I have been going to the local Ainu language school for the last 10 years or so, and actually I am the chair of the steering committee of the school. Mr. Shigeru Kayano (1926 – 2006), the founder of the language school, asked me to become the chair about a year before he passed away. I felt uncomfortable about the job because I was not really a 'native' speaker. So, I declined the offer, saying that I would not like to cause an unnecessary trouble. Mr. Kayano then said that the Ainu Language School needed to exist, and someone had to become the chair. He told me that I could learn the language myself at the school with the students and serve the Ainu community as well."

Figure 63 A classroom at the Ainu Language School in Biratori. The school offers classes for children and adults (2014).

[137] *Japan Studies Review* originally published this section as an article. See Ito 2014a. I added more information for this book.

[138] Ito. *Have You Heard about the Ainu?* 2015.

Kazunobu has been adamant about learning and practicing Ainu in his later years. He has particularly focused on learning the Ainu hero epics and ballads for the last 15 years. He said, "Recently, I won an award for singing an Ainu folk ballad, in one of the contests in Sapporo," and he showed me the certificate that he was presented with. In 2011, he was awarded a certificate of gratitude. It was for his contributions to the preservation, transmission, and promotion of Ainu culture by the Organization for Promotion of Ainu Culture and Studies.

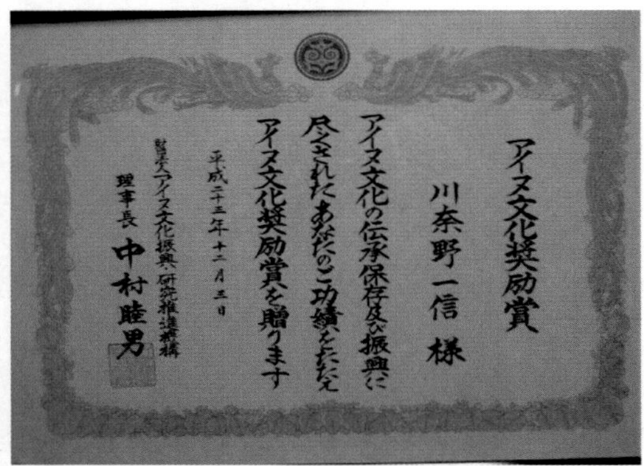

アイヌ文化奨励賞

川奈野一信 様

アイヌ文化の伝承保存及び振興に尽くされたあなたのご功績をたたえアイヌ文化奨励賞を贈ります

平成二十三年十二月三日

アイヌ文化振興・研究推進機構

理事長 中村睦男

Figure 64 Mr. Kawanano's award certificate from the Foundation for Research and Promotion of Ainu Culture for his efforts in transmission, preservation, and promotion of the Ainu culture.

In 2011 and 2012, the Foundation for Research and Promotion of Ainu Culture honored and awarded Kazunobu for his excellent performance in the Ainu speech contest on oral literature. He also received an award for promotion of Ainu culture from the Biratori Town's Board of Education.

Figure 65 Mr. Kawanano is holding an award certificate from the Foundation for Research and Promotion of Ainu Culture for the 15th Ainu language speech contest.

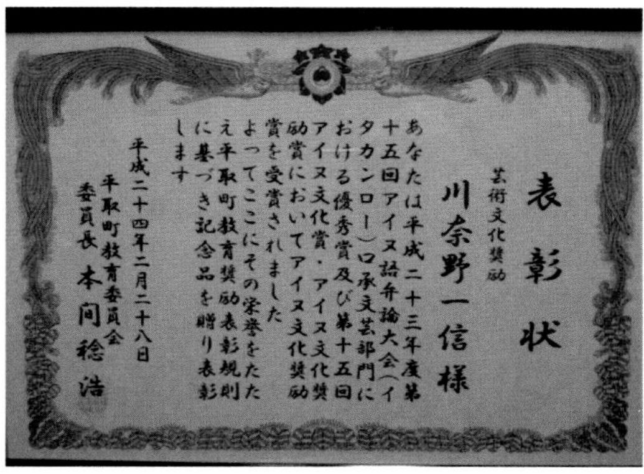

表彰状

芸術文化奨励

川奈野一信様

あなたは平成二十三年度第
十五回アイヌ語弁論大会（イ
タカンロー）口承文芸部門に
おける優秀賞及び第十五回
アイヌ文化賞・アイヌ文化奨
励賞においてアイヌ文化奨励
賞を受賞されました
よってここにその栄誉をたた
え平取町教育奨励表彰規則
に基づき記念品を贈り表彰
します

平成二十四年二月二十八日

平取町教育委員会
委員長 本間稔浩

Figure 66 An award certificate from Biratori's Board of Education praising Mr. Kawanano's performance of Ainu oral literature.

Kazunobu's father excelled in reading and writing in his elementary school. Upon graduation, he started working as an apprentice at a major liquor store owned by a *Wajin* (non-Ainu ethnic majority Japanese) in town, which also served as a small post office. He worked as a store clerk and mail carrier. He had to deliver mail on foot or on a bicycle to places that were 15 to 20 kilometers (approximately 9.4 to 12.5 miles) away, and the roads had many hills. Later he married Kazunobu's mother, Toshi. She was from the same town and was the last of five children in her family. They had two sons together, Kazunobu and his younger brother.

The owner of the store, who was a *Wajin*, said to Kazunobu's father one day, "You have been working very diligently, and I will give you land. Go there, clear it, cultivate the land, and engage in agriculture. You can be independent." Kazunobu was about two years of age when his family left town to make their home on this given land, which was further inland where large trees and weeds were lush.

Kazunobu said, "My father cut the large trees, dug roots, and did his best to cultivate the land, but we suffered a lot financially. He was no longer receiving wages from the liquor store. We had nothing, no money, no food, nothing! We would go to a nearby brook, fill two buckets with water, and bring them back to the house on the opposite ends of a wooden bar over the shoulders. We stored it in a *miso* barrel.[139] We used the water for drinking and cooking, but by today's sanitation standard, it would be considered harmful to your health."

The Japanese immigrants brought new diseases to which the Ainu did not have immunity. Many of them died of tuberculosis, measles, and sexually transmitted diseases due to the lack of immunity. The situation was very similar to that of the original inhabitants in the United States, Latin America, and elsewhere. Kazunobu's father was no exception. He caught tuberculosis when Kazunobu was four years old.

Kazunobu said, "Tuberculosis was rather common in those days among the Ainu and the *Wajin*. There was not much mechanization in agriculture then, and people had to keep working very hard without proper nutrition. Many suffered from pneumonia and tuberculosis. My father could not afford to go see a doctor. My grandmother was an old-fashioned Ainu woman, and she knew a lot about folk medicine and remedies. Her knowledge included various herbs, trees, and utilization of their seeds, leaves, roots, fruits, and sap. She gave him herbs and barks in hot water, yet my father died in April when I was six years old."

Kazunobu commented that adequate housing was also a problem in his early life. He said, "Our old house looked worse than the stables or huts where the cows, horses, or dogs lived.

[139] Miso is fermented soybean paste used for sauce, soup, pickling, and seasoning in Japanese cuisine.

Looking back at those days, I really wonder how we survived in that house and maintained our health. We did not have indoor plumbing just like many other traditional Ainu houses, and in the summer time, we went to the river. We did not bathe in the winter. I did not have any shoes and went barefooted to school, to play, or to the mountains to pick grapes. Sometimes pieces of broken glass bottles were on the road, and I injured my foot. In the wintertime, snow and ice would come through the holes in the walls of our house, and it was very cold. I wore shoes made of leather to school in wintertime. We called those shoes *keri*, and they were made of either horse or pigskin. I put old rags around my feet, and then wore *keri* shoes. By the time I arrived at school, my shoes were frozen. I dried my shoes near the stove. Once you wear them, they became soft and no longer hard. We made those shoes at home."

He continued with his memories. He said, "There used to be a lot of horses in those days – rich families had a few to dozens of horses to help them with farming and pulling down lumber from the mountains. When a horse died, we made *keri* shoes with the skin and ate the meat. Now there are regulations for butchering meat, but in those days, we just ate it. We did not have good food, my father was overworked, and he ended up dying young with tuberculosis. I can remember my father only very vaguely because I was not even in elementary school when he passed."

Lumber and charcoal production used to be two of the major industries of Biratori, and horse-drawn wagons shipped lumber for sale when Kazunobu was young. The *Wajin* cut trees as they pleased and made charcoal as an occupation in those days. Several Ainu men told me in 2012 how they used to deplore the naked mountains after all the trees were cut and sold. Luckily, there has been a social and political movement to restore the mountains to the original state, and they have been successful.

Figure 67 A model of a horse-drawn wagon that carried lumber from the mountains (Photo by the author: courtesy of the Historical Museum of Saru River).

"My mother, Toshi, had to work after she became a widow in her 20s, maybe she was like 27. I think my grandmother was in her 50s by then, and she went to work with my mother as *dementori*, day laborers on farms. My younger brother and I were on our own while they were gone, and I followed their instructions regarding what to eat for lunch since the age of seven or eight. I cleaned the lamps, cooked, and did other things, so I can still do them.

"I was the first-born and had to take care of my younger brother, and I took him to school with me, too. I, just like many other Ainu children in those days, and even today to a certain extent, was bullied and discriminated against at school on many days by my *Wajin* teacher and classmates. They looked down on me just because I was an Ainu. I went to an elementary school in the Osachinai District in town where there were a lot of Ainu families. Many of the schoolchildren's fathers engaged in charcoal production in the mountains. These *Wajin* families would stay in the region for five, or maybe six years, and they moved around like nomads. The local people, both the Ainu and *Wajin*, did not discriminate against us, but these *Wajin* children of charcoal makers would ridicule us as being dirty, hairy, and smelling like urine even though they were no better off than we were. I was very strong when it came to fighting. The *Wajin* schoolteacher carried a cane-looking bar, which was about 1 yard and 4 inches in length. He would always say that I was in the wrong in a fight or an argument just because I was an Ainu, and then beat me with the stick. The *Wajin* children thought that we Ainu were always in the wrong when we were not. Therefore, they justified and escalated their bullying of us. The *Wajin* children repeatedly bullied me at school. Of course, I was not the only one who was bullied and scolded.

The *Wajin* children used to call us "You, Ainu!" in a derogatory manner and say things like "*A inu ga kita*" ("Ah, a 'dog' is coming)" when we approached them. In Japanese *inu* means "a dog" and the word Ainu is divided into two words: *a* + *inu* ("Ah" and "dog"). This idea that the Ainu are inferior beings, and bad, let me down. I was not motivated to learn the Ainu language when I was young. I did not even try to learn, even though my grandmother spoke Ainu with her friends all the time. My mother did not speak Ainu in front of me. However, their voices speaking Ainu still sound in my ears since I heard them speaking Ainu to one another."

Both the *Wajin* teachers and children made Kazunobu feel miserable at school, and he had low self-esteem. However, it did not last forever. He said, "A new principal came to our school when I was in the 5th grade. He was an exceptionally good principal. There was no more discrimination against me, or bullying me after he came. All the students got along and became friends."

The contemporary Ainu, just like their ancestors, refer to non-Ainu ethnic majority Japanese as *Wajin*. I heard this word very often in their daily conversations among both the Ainu and the *Wajin* while I was doing research in Biratori in 2011, 2012, and 2014. It seems to me that the Ainu-*Wajin*, or the "us" vs. "them," dichotomy characterizes one of the most basic elements of one's identity, social status and relation, and label in Biratori. This dichotomy popped up in many conversations when both groups are talking about each other among themselves. The Ainu people use *Wajin* to refer to non-Ainu ethnic majority Japanese. I personally have never heard any non-Ainu Japanese person using the word *Wajin*, neither in Honshu, since there is no need to differentiate the term *Nihonjin* (Japanese) and *Wajin* among themselves.

The derogatory form for *Wajin* is *shamo*. Interestingly enough, I found *shamo* used as often as the word *Wajin* among the Ainu in their daily conversations, especially among the older Ainu men. The *Wajin* interviewees of mine, both male and female, also engaged in derogatory comments about the Ainu and their life styles as well when the Ainu were not present.

Kazunobu continued, "When we moved to K District in town it was not the students but the *Wajin* teachers who bullied us Ainu kids more. They would not even come near us because they thought we were filthy, and it was always us, the Ainu kids, who were beaten up. I experienced it, but I saw many other Ainu children who were bullied more than I was.

"I envied those Ainu children who were half-Ainu and half-*Wajin*, because looking more like *Wajin* reduced the amount of ridicule and bullying. The bullies would not really think that these kids were Ainu, either. They think that they were *Wajin* and never called them 'Ainu! Ainu!' like they did to us. Unfortunately, the *Wajin* used the word Ainu, which means humans in the Ainu language, as a word of contempt, a derogatory term. Actually, the Ainu Association of

Hokkaido changed its name to the *Utari* (compatriot) Association in 1961 because of this negative association and then changed its name back to the Ainu Association in 2009.

"When I was young, so many Japanese from different parts of Honshu moved to Hokkaido looking for a better life. Japan was still a very poor nation, and people had a very difficult time. However, many immigrants did not fare well; they were not at all prepared for the harsh winter here. They suffered from hunger and cold temperatures. They lived in primitive huts. When they decided to leave Hokkaido and go back to Honshu, they left their infants with Ainu families just like those Japanese parents who left their infants and children to the Chinese at the end of World War II. They could barely go back to Japan themselves. This abandoning of their children and entrusting them to the hands of strangers was one of the ways to save their young lives. Those *Wajin* babies who were brought up by their Ainu foster parents spoke the Ainu language, followed the Ainu traditions, and believed their myths, and they became the Ainu of the Ainus even though they appeared to be *Wajin*.

"My Ainu friend, Mr. Nabesawa, looks like a *Wajin*. His mother was an infant left by her Japanese parents. Her Ainu parents brought her up, and she married an Ainu. Last year my friend Nabesawa was in charge of a particular traditional Ainu ceremony. Many people there asked me whether he was really an Ainu or not, because he inherited his facial features from his *Wajin* mother. His grandmother spoke only the Ainu language, and Nabesawa lived with her until he was 17 years old. Thus, Nabesawa can speak Ainu very fluently. I think he is just about the only one who is a native speaker among the Ainu men around here.

"In our district, there were a lot of Japanese immigrants from places like Sendai or Niigata, and they engaged in agriculture. As a good friend of mine used to say, they came to Hokkaido like an avalanche, occupied the land, and they took all the fertile land away from the Ainu, and started farming and developing. The Ainu did not have their own nation; our language does not have letters, and my ancestors lived in harmony with nature. The *Wajin* 'gave' the native Ainu barren, very poor land, told them to cultivate it themselves, and forced them to live there as farmers. The government did not give the Ainu much land anyway, and our ancestors were hunters, anglers, and gatherers, and not really farmers. They became poorer and poorer, especially during bad harvests.

"Many Ainu men loved to drink, and some were in debt due to their heavy drinking. In those days, they had a system in which customers would buy goods at a store on credit. The storeowner would record the amount of the purchases, and the customers would pay the total amount of the bill on a specific date sometime later. Some Ainu men, who happened to be totally drunk, would walk around in town smelling like alcohol and come to this liquor store. The storeowner, knowing that the drunkards would not remember anything, would write in their credit records that these unsuspecting Ainu 'purchased' some liquor on that day. Later, he would demand payment in full. The drunkards could not remember anything or defend themselves. The *Wajin* storeowner made a lot of money this way, and when the Ainu said that he could not pay the bill, the owner would demand that he pay in land. If the Ainu did not have land, a mountain would do. The Ainu lost a lot due to their notorious drunkenness due to the *Wajin*'s corrupt system of buying with credit.

"Among the immigrant Japanese farming families, there were the T and A families who were excellent and very rich farmers. I had a few classmates who were about the same age in my neighborhood; they were a son or a daughter of these very rich families. They were wonderful people and treated me and often my brother, too, to delicious food. I am still friends with one of them like brothers. I also had a friend whose parents came from Sendai, and his family grew rice, the only one who did so in the community. One day, a classmate of mine invited me to his house, which was huge. I was very hesitant to enter through the main entrance. Even though I was a small child, I knew I was dirty and stinky. Mr. T, my classmate's father, told me to go to the back door, take off my shoes, and enter the house from there. They knew that my family was very poor and offered me a lot of food, saying 'You must be hungry. Eat as much as you want. Eat until you get full and then go home.' I ate a bowl of white rice for the first time in my life that day. I still remember how delicious it was."

Kazunobu continued, "Our family lived on potatoes, *kabocha* (pumpkins), barnyard millet, millet, and so on in those days. I had millet for lunch at school. It does not have the stickiness. When it is warm, it is pretty good, but once it gets cold it becomes very dry like rice bran. In those days, lunch boxes were oval-shaped and made of metal. All the students warmed the boxes on the stove in the classroom. When I tried to get my lunch box with my bare hands one day, it was so hot that I dropped it on the floor. The millet spread all over the floor, and I could not eat it. I had to throw it away.

"When I was in the 4th grade, I was able to help my mother and grandmother by weeding in our very small vegetable garden in front of the humble house and gathering firewood in the mountains. I also worked on a farm to earn money. I had to weed in the soybean or adzuki fields that were 100 or 200 meters (approximately 109-219 yards) long. Since I was only a child, I could not keep up with the adult workers, and many women helped me catch up with them. The wages were two *shō* (@3.6 liters) of dried corn. We were living from hand to mouth, and we did not have much to eat. In the wintertime, we ate preserved *kabocha* pumpkins that we harvested in the autumn and dried in the sun. As soon as I arrived home from my farm work, I ground the dried corn in a mortar called *iyuta*. Two people can pound the grain in the mortar easily, but three can pound at the same time, too. It is a bit more difficult that way, and I am the only one who can still do it. Anyway, when my mother came home to find the gruel made with ground grains (corn, millet, etc.), she used to commend me and say 'You are great!' and it made me feel very happy." Kazunobu found joy in pleasing his mother and grandmother by working hard and contributing to the family economy.

"My mother remarried Mr. Ueda, a Japanese man from Niigata who came to Hokkaido to work when I was 11 years old. Mr. Ueda and my mother had two sons. My stepfather said that he would take care of me and my brother, but he would let us keep our last name in due respect to our late Ainu father. He was a great stepfather. He was very gentle and loved my brother and me genuinely. He did not have any prejudice toward the Ainu people. We were still poor, but our new life with Mother and the stepfather began. Mr. Ueda did many things for me, and his assistance reduced my household labors, like going to mountains and making firewood.

"My stepfather had relatives in Sapporo and Otaru, and he used to go there to visit them several times a year. When I was in the 6th grade, he went to Sapporo and brought me back a new set of skis. In those days, skis were very rare, and even children from rich families did not have them. All my friends were envious of me, and many people asked where I got them. They begged me to let them touch or use them. I felt very lucky to have Mr. Ueda as my stepfather.

"In the fall of 1945 or so, my maternal grandfather gave my mother some land, and we moved to a small rural community called Penakori. Mr. Ueda built a hut with the logs that he had cut and brought from the mountain. He also purchased and used cheap wood boards, which had not met the industry standard, from a sawmill. Snow and wind came in through the holes in the walls and under the eaves during winter. We needed to put up wood boards to cover the holes. My mother and stepfather worked very hard every day, but our life was not easy. I tried to help them out, and I went to a farm to work and make some money. I went to junior high school for two years, but in my third year, I went to work in the mountains cutting grass and trees, and transporting logs on the river and making lumber. Because of this, I could not attend enough days at junior high school, and I did not receive a diploma. Many Ainu were in the same position. When the junior high school celebrated its 100th year anniversary, my name was entered into the registration of graduates though.

"Mr. Ueda concluded that his family could not keep living in poverty and decided to apply for new land and engage in agriculture around 1955. He bought land in Kaminukibetsu thanks to an order that allowed people without land to purchase some cheaply. If they were successful in cultivation and could pass an inspection within five years, the land became theirs to keep. Our plot was about 30 km (approximately 19 miles) from our house. My stepbrothers were still very young, and my parents took the youngest son with them to work since he was not healthy. I took care of my brother and stepbrother while my parents were away. They would take two to three hours every day to commute in a horse buggy on the mountain roads. They needed to cut trees without machinery, and it was a very hard labor to cultivate the land. I would ride my bicycle with my brother and helped my parents there, too.

"The work in the lush land was excruciatingly difficult. It is beyond a normal person's imagination. There were huge trees and weeds were everywhere. My stepfather also engaged in charcoal production in the mountain. He built a kiln, burned wood, and sold the charcoal to special charcoal sellers to earn a living. After several years, when the land had finally been cultivated, my stepfather suffered from cancer. He died a year later, in 1972. He was 60-some years old. He loved his children and grandchildren. My youngest stepbrother inherited the land and business. Today he has 23 green houses and his business is doing very well.

Figure 68 Farmers grow tomatoes in green houses, one of the famous products of the town.

"In my teenage years, the only jobs available were related to the lumber business; cutting trees, transporting logs on the river, making lumber, etc. I stayed and did various kinds of work in the mountains for months and months. We loaded logs into trucks, which delivered them to paper mills or woodworking plants. In the winter, my hands often froze, and they turned white. However, I kept working because it was my boss's order. In those days, you must always obey the orders from an adult who was your boss, and older. I worked very hard not to be scolded. Later, I purchased a horse and worked in the mountains because I could make more money with my own horse.

"I got married to Motoko when I was 24 in 1959. Motoko and I have known each other for a long time, since our childhood. In those days, dating was not common here. You may not be able to believe it, but things like dating did not exist," Kazunobu said.

"How did you meet her?" I asked him.

"I really did not know her. It happened more than 50 years ago," Kazunobu replied.

"You don't remember!?" I said.

"Not really. We lived in the same village, and we knew each other by sight. In those days, we were not even thinking about marriage. I am 7 years older than Motoko. Well, for some reason, I was very popular with the girls since my youth. I am serious. I really did not know how to pick a wife, but I thought I liked Motoko best. Both of us had a difficult childhood without a father. The two of us shared similar circumstances. We felt like birds of a feather and could understand each other. When you are young, you marry without thinking about the meaning. I don't think people calculate everything and then marry," Kazunobu said.

Kazunobu and Motoko had celebrated their golden anniversary, and I asked him about the secret for successful marriage.

"(Friendly) fighting. The most common reason for fighting has to do with too little money. In those days, everyone was poor. Nevertheless, we naturally overcame the problems just like everyone else. I didn't know why at the time, but we ended up with six kids. My wife suffered the most. Raising kids is tough! Husbands tend to be less responsible around the house. Men think it is good enough to earn money for the family and not worry about the wife and the kids. Women suffer when men act that way. Women in these days can get divorced easily, but in those days, people did not get divorced. We thought it normal that we would have difficulties because we are poor, or in raising children. Anyway, you need to take good care of women. Old Ainu people used to say that 'A home without a fire and a woman is a lonely house,'" Kazunobu observed.

As the interview continued, I also asked Motoko how she felt about marrying Kazunobu. She said, "I fell in love with my husband because I thought that his family grew rice, and this meant I would probably not go hungry again."

Motoko's father, according to her, was "half Ainu and half *Wajin*." He also died young like Kazunobu's father. Her mother was a *Wajin* from Sapporo whom an Ainu couple adopted when she was four. Her adoptive parents had always spoken in the Ainu language, but Motoko's mother spoke only Japanese in front of her children, which was typical of parents in those days. Motoko's mother did speak Ainu with her friends. Her mother had many siblings, one of who found where she lived, and they later introduced themselves and kept in touch as a family.

Kazunobu continued, "Motoko and I had six children; four boys and two girls. It did not make sense for me that I always stay in the mountains leaving my family in town. I decided to get a truck driver's license so that I could commute to work and stay with my family every day. I told my wife, 'It could be tough while I am going to driver's school in Tomakomai, but when I become a truck driver I can stay with you.'

"I purchased a big truck and worked as a driver for a very long time. I loaded gravel and sand onto my truck and drove to Sapporo just about every day. I would get up at two or three o'clock in the morning and go back and forth to Sapporo a few times a day. It was a time of very high economic growth in Japan and construction companies needed sand and gravel to build tall buildings and roads."

Figure 69 Mrs. Motoko Kawanano with their pet Moe.

Sapporo is the capitol city of Hokkaido, which is a very modern metropolis. The population is 1.97 million people as of August 2018.[140] The city hosted the 11th Olympic Winter Games in 1972, the first Winter Games held in Japan and Asia. According to Henshall, Japanese annual GNP grew around 9% in the 1950s, 10% in the early 1960s, and to more than 13% in the late 1960s and early 1970s[141].

Kazunobu kept reminiscing about his job. He said, "In winter, this truck driving job got scarce due to snow, so I went to Kisarazu or Kimitsu in Chiba Prefecture in Honshu to work and make money. I went there every year from January to the 'Golden Week'[142] in May. I drove my dump truck through Tomakomai, Hachinohe, and then Tokyo where jobs were abundant. I worked at Tokyo Bay to fill the land. I did that for 20 years until 2007. Even though I lived there in the wintertime, 20 years is a long time, and I know Kisarazu and Kimitsu very well. Without that job, I do not think we could have built this house. We do not have any mortgage payment, but we only have *Kokumin Nenkin* (National Social Security). From now on, it will be difficult because the government is going to reduce the amount of payment. The politicians are trying to increase the tax rates now, too. Japan will sink in the future, you know! It will."

Kazunobu has been very active in many Ainu cultural activities since the 1970s. He said, "In 1970, I became the director of the Hokkaido Ainu Association's local branch and served more than 40 years. I am also the vice president of our Ainu Culture Preservation Association and the chair of the steering committee of the Ainu Language School in Biratori. I have been active in a project called 'Restoring *Iwor*.' *Iwor* is a traditional and ecological living space, and it entails biological resources in the area. The Ainu traditionally do not have a notion of private land ownership. Land belongs to their community."

His mother Toshi Ueda contributed much to the preservation of the Ainu oral tradition. Kazunobu told me about his mother's greatest accomplishment as a storyteller. He said, "My mother was born in October, 1912 in Penakori near Nibutani (in Biratori Town). It was a community where the majority were of Ainu descent. Both of her parents were Ainu. She always worked very hard to support the family. She handed the agricultural business to my stepbrother after my stepfather passed away. She then got involved with Mr. Shigeru Kayano's project to preserve the Ainu language.

---

[140] www.city.sapporo.jp/toukei/jinko/jinko.html. Accessed 9/2/18.

[141] Kenneth Henshell. 2004, pp.157-158.

[142] The Golden Week refers to the cluster of national holidays on April 29th (Showa Day), May 3rd (Constitution Day), May 4th (Green Day), and May 5th (Children's Day) and a Saturday and a Sunday.

"My mother was 64 or 65 years old years old, and she could not speak the Ainu language at the time. However, she used to live with her grandparents who spoke Ainu until she became an adult. At her house, her parents, especially her father, did not like her to speak Ainu like many other Ainu parents who wanted their children to grow up to be Japanese. Those parents made a difficult decision to abandon their Ainu tradition to prevent the occurrence of bullying or discrimination against their children at school or in society in those days.

"Luckily, my mother still remembered Ainu words, and they came back to her as Mr. Kayano talked to her in Ainu. Her elder sister Kimi Kimura also cooperated with Mr. Kayano, and my mother started to go to her sister's house by bus to learn Ainu stories in the early 1980s. She wanted to write down the old stories, but her sister told her to remember them by rote memory. After her sister passed away, my mother was determined to pass on the Ainu language even more. By the mid-1990s, my mother became an expert in the Ainu language, especially in telling *Uepeker* and *Yukar*," Kazunobu said.

Uepeker and *Yukar* are forms of narratives in Ainu. *Uepeker* refers to the old folktales told in everyday language. A storyteller of *Uepeker* becomes a protagonist such as an animal or an ordinary person and tells the audience his or her circumstances, various experiences, skills and wisdom for everyday life, precepts, and lessons. *Yukar* is an epic poem in the form of verse. Talented storytellers perform it rhythmically by tapping the edge of the fireplace with a wooden stick called *repni*. The stories are extraordinary, and the protagonists are Ainu gods or heroes. The so-called "elegant language" tells the stories[143].

"My mother used to say, 'I had difficult times in my life, but thanks to Kayano-sensei, I had a very good life. It is also thanks to my children who were not ashamed of being Ainu. I would not have done it if they were opposed to it.' Many Ainu children and adult children sometimes do not like it when their parents get involved with things Ainu due to shame, but my brothers and I were different. It was one of her favorite things to do, and we thought she should do it.

"My mother died at the age of 93 in 2005, but 5 or 6 years prior to her death, she had many opportunities to speak Ainu and present *Yukar* and *Uepeker* in Osaka, Nagoya, and Hakodate and Kushiro in Hokkaido. I think her case was rather rare to travel to so many places by air. It was really thanks to Mr. Kayano's kindness that she could do that as an Ainu woman."

Mrs. Toshi Ueda, Kazunobu's mother, is indeed well known as an Ainu *Uepeker* teller, and her performances were compiled into books and CDs. Japanese researchers use her stories and performances for their linguistic analysis. Mrs. Ueda also cooperated with the museums and researchers and helped them with recording and collection of data and information. Her *Uepeker of the Saru Region Transmitted by Toshi Ueda* was published by the Foundation for Research and Promotion of Ainu Culture. She was awarded *the Hokkaido Bunkazaihogo Kōrōsha Award* (a person who rendered distinguished service to the preservation of cultural properties) for her dedication and hard work in 1996.

Kazunobu told me many times that he is very happy that he is an Ainu. I asked him why. He said, "I had to endure many hardships, but I also benefitted a lot from my membership in the Ainu Association, and I can really say that I am glad I am an Ainu now. We built this house more than 30 years ago. You can borrow up to 7,200,000 yen (approximately US$65,500) to build your house, and start paying a mere 2 percent mortgage rate in the following year. This is a lot lower than other mortgages. If you need to get a driver's license, you will get 50,000 yen (approximately US$455) since a driver's license is a necessity to earn money for living. If you

[143] Yoichi Tsunoda. 2018, pp.184-185.

are an angler and need a boating license, it is the same. My children benefitted from scholarships, too. For example, when a student enters a senior high school, scholarships are given three times a year, and the same for college students. You need to return the money you are awarded if you drop out, though." I would like to add here that one of my informants in her 20s told me that this scholarship might be causing jealousy among the *Wajin* students, and lead to their bullying the Ainu students.

There are other benefits to the Ainu when it comes to state funding. Kazunobu said to me, "The Japanese government helps with building sewage disposal system facilities and pays about 70 to 90 percent of the cost. This program is part of improving the living conditions of the Ainu residents, and of course, the *Wajin* residents benefit from it, too, since they live in the same neighborhood. The money that the Ainu Association received from the Japanese government also supported paving the roads in neighborhoods where many Ainu lived. In order to preserve Ainu culture, money is available for those who teach and learn Ainu crafts. As for me, when I go to elementary schools and teach how to grow agricultural products, I am paid 5,400 yen (@US$50) per hour. They do direct deposit. My brother who owns greenhouses also gets money, and the *Wajin* farmers benefit from this help as well. Thanks to the money given to the Ainu, both the Ainu and *Wajin* residents in the whole community can thrive.

"I think the prefecture of Hokkaido has the attitude that they want to cherish Ainu culture, which I think is good. Hokkaido used to belong to the Ainu, yet our history is full of exploitation and oppression. I became friends with Mr. Kayano, a very influential Ainu man who became the first Ainu national assembly member. He invited me to come along with him to different places in Honshu such as Tokyo, Osaka, Matsusaka, Akita, and Yamagata as well as abroad, to Canada, South Korea, and New Zealand, to promote mutual awareness among the ethnic minorities of the world. I feel very lucky to have travelled to these countries as a representative of the Ainu."

On March 11, 2011, huge earthquakes and many tsunamis hit the northeast Tohoku Region of Japan, and the Fukushima nuclear disaster also took place. Kazunobu commented on what was going on at that time. He said, "The Japanese are now discriminating against these people from Fukushima. I would say that the radioactivity would not be contagious. The person from Fukushima who is visiting us here in Hokkaido will not contaminate us, or the land. Some people misunderstand this, and certain gas stations have signs saying 'No Cars from Fukushima Served.' This is horrible. Yesterday's paper reported it. That is awful."

I visited the Kawananos again in the summer of 2012. Kazunobu said that it is very important for me to record their stories not only in my words but also on a video camera so that people can hear and see them talk from their own mouths and not from a researcher's writings. He said, "We are old and can die anytime now. I want you to document us the next time you come to town." He was 78 years old at that time. Oddly enough, an elderly Ainu man nicknamed Fuku-chan, who was 76 years old, passed away only six months after my visit.

Kazunobu said that the old Ainu people could not wait for the NHK (Nippon Hoso Kyokai, an equivalent of the BBC of the Great Britain in Japan) to come to town and make their documentary films. Kazunobu inspired me, which led to my obtaining another scholarship from the Dean's office to go there and make a film in 2014.

In 2014, the Indian government invited Kazunobu and other Ainu people from Biratori to engage in the cultural exchange programs. I asked him about his trip. He said, "For an old man like me, India was so far away. We flew from Sapporo to Tokyo, and then to New Delhi. We were always busy moving from one city to another by air and by bus. It was worth it. We enjoyed performing for the Indian audience, and we had a very good cultural exchange programs."

Chapter 7: Mr. Nabesawa: My Ainu "Professor"

I first met Mr. Tamotsu Nabesawa and his wife in 2012. They graciously let me stay in their home for four days. Mr. Nabesawa took me to various places in town that had significance in his life as an Ainu during the day. In the evening, Mrs. Nabesawa let me help her in her kitchen and kindly showed me how to prepare seafood and vegetables. She cooked delicious meals using the freshest ingredients and served us dinner very happily. I was quite impressed with her hospitality. She said, "My parents back in Honshu were farmers, and we lived in a very big house with many rooms. We cultivated rice and kept horses. My parents belonged to a large Buddhist sect, and we always had visitors, some of who were the followers of their sect. They would stay in our house for a week. Thus, I am used to cooking and serving people."

Mr. Nabesawa invited a few of his Ainu friends to dinner, and their interesting stories entertained me every night. After dinner, we usually discussed the Ainu, and we talked about various topics – their everyday life, history, social policies, and religion, just to name a few. I was very happy about the many opportunities that Mr. and Mrs. Nabesawa provided me during my stay. I was fortunate to ask Mr. Nabesawa and his Ainu friends many questions. Mr. Nabesawa knew so much about the Ainu, their history, culture, traditions, and hardships. He was like a university professor and was always more than willing to share his experiences as an Ainu.

Figure 70 The Modern Nabesawa Residence.

Figure 71 A delicious dinner at the Nabesawas – fresh fish and vegetables.

Figure 72 Fresh scallops that Mrs. Nabesawa's niece sent. Mrs. Nabesawa told me that all parts are edible, which I did not know.

We talked until late at night in a more relaxed atmosphere, especially after Mr. Nabesawa offered his friends some beer or *sake*. I took many notes as if I was attending a lecture at a university, and my right hand got so stiff at the end that I could barely write. I am not a drinker at all, but I was very happy to gather rich ethnographical data in a more informal and joyous atmosphere where some people became inebriated and more open. When the clock struck midnight, Mr. Nabesawa said, "I am going to the land of dreams now. Good night, everyone!" I said, "Thank you so much" and "*Oyasuminasai* (Good night)!" to him, his wife, and friends.

Mr. Tamotsu Nabesawa was born in 1936. His father was an Ainu, and his mother was an ethnic Ainu. She was a *Wajin* (non-Ainu ethnic majority Japanese) adopted by an Ainu couple when she was an infant. Mr. Nabesawa takes after his mother and can easily pass as a *Wajin*.

Figure 73 Mr. Tamotsu Nabesawa in front of his greenhouses (2012).

Mr. Nabesawa is one of the very few native speakers of Ainu who can speak with great fluency in Biratori Town, or possibly, in the prefecture of Hokkaido and all Japan today. His historical, social, and linguistic knowledge of the Ainu is vast, and I felt extremely fortunate to interview him. I asked him the reason why he could speak the language so fluently.

Mr. Nabesawa said, "I lived with my paternal grandmother who spoke only Ainu. Luckily, she lived to be an old woman. She had a very long life by the longevity standard of the day. I lived with her until I was 17 years old. In those days when I was a child and could not write, say, between the ages of three and six, I started to recognize that each Ainu word she spoke had a different meaning. That was how I mastered the language."

Non-verbal communication is also very important to the Ainu. Mr. Nabesawa said, "When an Ainu person greets another Ainu, he uses not only words but also gestures. Here is the problem. How do you understand the greetings that come with a certain gesture? Only a video camera can record the full spectrum of this kind of greeting." Mr. Nabesawa showed me how to say greetings using both hands in addition to making the sounds. He added, "When you just read this greeting in a written language, the nuance of the greeting cannot be conveyed without the gesture." For example, an Ainu greeting of welcoming and sending off guests entails holding each other's hands, hugging, and tapping on the shoulder.

Figure 74 Mr. Nabesawa is teaching Ainu greetings to the author.

Figure 75 We finished the greeting with a hug.

The Ainu language does not have a writing system, and the Ainu thus have very strong oral traditions. In those days when there were no radios, televisions, or internet the Ainu children used to listen to their elders talk by the fireside for entertainment and socialization to make them law-abiding group members. That was how the Ainu transmitted their history, language, tradition, wisdom, and culture to the next generation.

Here is Mr. Nabesawa's story:

"My grandmother's name was Sietakutaku. *Sie* in the Ainu language means 'poop' and *takutaku* means 'to coat' or 'to paint.' Thus, her name literally means she is 'coated with poop.' She was very weak when she was born, and her parents wanted her to be strong and healthy. They loved the baby so much that they gave her such an unthinkable name. The Ainu traditionally believed that such a name would prevent an evil spirit or demon from getting near her. My grandmother, maybe thanks to her name, lived to be 86 or 87 years old. She did not lose her mental capacity, either. She was healthy and alert. Her parents' wishes did come true.

"Sietakutaku got married to a *Wajin* when she was 20 years old or so. She changed her name to Tekeirimat, which meant 'a person who has excellent skills.' She had sewing talents and excelled in embroidery. She used to make threads out of tree bark fiber for weaving mats as she kept talking with me by the fireside.

"My mother had a very interesting fate. It is like a novel. I do not know much about my mother's background because an Ainu family adopted her when she was a newborn baby. She did not know her birth mother. I only know that my maternal grandparents were *Wajin*. Many *Wajin* immigrated to Hokkaido in those days, and I am not quite sure if my grandfather used to be a *tondenhei*. I know that he was in the construction business and worked as a carpenter up north."

Tondenhei were soldiers who came to Hokkaido with their family members. The Japanese government gave them a house and land. *Hei* means "soldier" but they were also troops who became settlers. The Meiji government started soliciting the ex-samurai class from all over Japan in 1885, and more than 2,900 households migrated to 13 villages in Hokkaido. More than 4,400 households of the commoners also applied for the position after the law changed in 1890. They lived in 24 different areas including inland. The length of their military service was limited to 20 years.[144] The *tondenhei*s' missions included guarding the frontier, protecting Hokkaido from the invasion of Russia, and cultivation of undeveloped land as well as construction of roads and bridges. Many *Wajin* also immigrated to Hokkaido to find their fortune in the frontier, engage in business, and become rich.

"My grandmother got married to a carpenter who loved to drink. In those days, not only parents but also older brothers and sisters had much more power in the household when it came to family affairs. Because of her husband's drinking problem, the family members made her get divorced from him. She was pregnant and gave birth to a girl. Her family considered that she would remarry someone eventually, and thought that this new baby, who later became my mother, would rather be a burden in finding a new spouse.

"The family decided to give up this newborn baby for adoption when she was only a week or so old. A boy, whose name was Mansuke, was in charge of bringing her from Teshio to Biratori. He was 16 years old. There were no modern highways then, and Mansuke carried the baby on his back and rode a horse. They camped out on the way except for one night when they stayed in a *hatago* (inn). The owner's wife had a baby, and she kindly nursed the baby. I am sure she had not had mother's warm milk for a long time. After three days of traveling, they arrived in Biratori on the fourth day. As I said, Mansuke had a hard time carrying her on his back. I am sure she must have peed on him.

---

[144] Kato & Wakazono. 2018, p.70.

Figure 76 Many horses worked as agricultural labor and transportation in those days. Modern agricultural equipment, cars and trucks replaced them. Nowadays some people in Hokkaido keep them as pets.

Figure 77 The Hidaka Region, where Biratori Town is located, is the largest breeding center for horses in Japan.

"At the beginning of the Taisho Period (1912-1926), there were horses that were so-called *dosanko*. As you know, *dosanko* means native of or to Hokkaido. My mother's parents put two suitcases that were about 70 or 80 cm long on both sides of the horse. Inside the suitcases were many new and beautiful kimono for ceremonies and everyday wear. My mother would wear them when she became an adult. A small Ainu community that had about ten people was right here. The leader was an elderly woman called Upas ("Snow"), a relative of our family. I am not too certain but she could be a relative of Mansuke. Anyway, she decided to adopt the newborn baby.

"Once Upas adopted her, she had a hard time raising her. She must have been more interested in the new clothes in the suitcases than raising the baby. Upas remembered that she herself lived in Sapporo until she was five years old. I assume that she was also a *Wajin* whom an Ainu family adopted. She left Sapporo and moved to this town. She had an Ainu tattoo around her mouth.

"A woman named Kiyay ("Light") gave birth a week or ten days before the arrival of my mother. Kiyay actually had a stillbirth and lost her baby. However, she still had milk. Kiyay said to Upas, 'If you are having a hard time with the baby, I will nurse and raise her.' My mother, being a newborn, did not have much hair then, and she was a *raurau*, which means 'a person without hair' in Ainu. I started to lose hair myself in my 30s," Mr. Nabesawa touched his head with his right hand and laughed.

"So, I can call you *raurau ekasi* (skin-headed elder)?" I joked with him.

"Yes, you can say that," Mr. Nabesawa replied to me laughing.

Mr. Nabesawa continued his story and said, "Anyway the relatives had much doubt about Kiyay, and they wondered, 'How can she raise the baby?' Kiyay said, 'I will do my best to raise her by all means. Absolutely!' Thus, my mother lucked out again, just like when she and Mansuke stayed at the inn in Asahikawa. Kiyay had lost her child a while ago, and she thought that this baby came to her as a substitute. Kiyay adopted my mother.

"When I was a teen, we often had an old man visit us. *Who is this old man? He is not our relative,* I thought. I wondered about his identity but did not pursue it. I later found that he was nobody but Mansuke, the boy who brought my mother (who was a newborn baby) to this town. I think he felt *philos* (brotherly love) toward her, and that is why he wanted to check on her occasionally. I thought that Mansuke was engaged in fishing near the shore or something. He brought the baby at the end of October. As I thought more about it, Japan was exporting mint to China in those days. The trade was lucrative, and I think Mansuke came from the northern part of Hokkaido to engage in mint cultivation here. Up in the north, it is too cold and frost happens at the end of October.

"My maternal grandmother remarried after she gave up her baby (my mother) for adoption. I assumed she had more children with her new husband. I wanted my mother to meet her half-brothers and half-sisters when I was around 30 years old. I asked the elders about their whereabouts but to no avail. I found out that my mother's adoptive family did not get her birth certificate. That means that she officially was non-existent. There was no way I could find my mother's siblings."

I asked Mr. Nabesawa why Ainu families adopted so many *Wajin* children in those days. He replied, "The *Wajin* immigrants came to Hokkaido in great numbers thanks to the Meiji Government's colonization policies. There were actually jungles here. The tall trees were lush, and even during the daytime, it was dark in the forests. The immigrants could barely eat, not to mention clear the forests successfully and develop the land. When the situation got worse, they left their children in the hands of the Ainu families and went back to Honshu.

"At the end of the Edo period and during the Meiji period, many *Wajin* came to Hokkaido after they heard the stories that one could easily strike it rich in Hokkaido. The mixing of blood started to take place. When the *Wajin* women got pregnant and the family could not raise the child, many of them opted to leave the child at the entrance to an Ainu house. The Ainu would raise the child as their own. Thus, the child had *Wajin* blood, but he grew up as Ainu.

"The Japanese colonialists, who came to Hokkaido, especially along the coast line, raped many Ainu women. Hokkaido and Australia were alike in those days in that the governments sent certain criminals to faraway places as a punishment. Some people simply escaped to Hokkaido for one reason or another. The Ainu women, even when they were raped and got pregnant, welcomed the children because they considered that the child is a divine gift."

I asked Mr. Nabesawa how one could know that someone is an Ainu. "You can tell by looking at the face. I have a *Wajin* face because of my blood. I take after my mother. However, I was brought up as Ainu just like my mother. You can also tell who is an Ainu by their last names. For example, the Ainu names include, Kawakami, Kawanano, Kaizawa, Nabesawa, Hirame, Hiramura, Kurokawa, Hikawa, and Kayano."

In April 2010, a Scottish organization invited Mr. Nabesawa to perform Ainu *Yukar*. He went to Scotland in October accompanied by Shiro Kayano, who is the son of the late Shigeru Kayano. Mr. Nabesawa performed in various cities and stayed in Edinburgh for one week. He came to know some people there, and he cooked and shared Ainu dishes with them. He especially loved the potato dish there. He said, "Just like here in Hokkaido, their potatoes were very tasty. I also enjoyed having questions asked about the Ainu. When I came back to Japan, I thanked all my ancestors for providing me with a safe trip."

"When you visited Scotland, did you feel you were a Japanese national?" I asked Mr. Nabesawa about his identity.

"When I am abroad, I do," he said.

"But when you are in Biratori, you are an Ainu," I said.

"Yes, right," he said.

"So, when you go abroad, do you have a double identity – an identity as an Ainu and also as a Japanese national?" I asked him.

"I only am 50% Ainu in regard to blood. Nevertheless, I strongly identity with Ainu. An Ainu family adopted my *Wajin* mother, and she had no Ainu blood. I do not look Ainu enough, and I have faced reverse discrimination by the Ainu. But my soul is Ainu," he said.

"I see. You can pass as *Wajin*, but you identify strongly with the Ainu," I said.

"When the Ainu and *Wajin* children have a fight, the *Wajin* teachers always blamed the Ainu children for starting it even when they did not. That was a case all the time. It happened in communities such as Nibutani, Furenai, Osachinai, and right here. When I was in an elementary school, the *Wajin* teachers discriminated against me. I had a very strong sense of friendship. So, when I saw an Ainu child being bulled in a fight, and even though I personally had nothing to do with it, I would willingly join the fight and beat up the *Wajin* children," Mr. Nabesawa said laughing.

"I understand that you were resentful of these *Wajin* teachers and children in your community, right?" I asked him.

"The Ainu never asked or invited the *Wajin* to come to the Ainu homeland. The *Wajin* working for the Tokugawa Shogunate were interested in the natural resources up here. Imperial Russians were also coming down from the north looking for ice-free ports. My Ainu ancestors had been living here already at that time. They definitely did not considered Ainu as human beings. If we were humans, then the *Wajin* should have consulted us regarding land. They never did. There were wars between the Ainu and the *Wajin* such as the wars of Kunashiri and Menashi. A war makes winners and losers. I want people to understand history correctly, without manipulation. I want to share my culture and strive for mutual understanding," Mr. Nabesawa said.

In August 1869, the Meiji government claimed Ezochi, Kunashiri Island, Etorofu Island, and other islands in the vicinity as a Japanese territory and renamed them Hokkaido. Ezochi included the land that "belonged to" the Matsumae Domain during the Tokugawa Period and the *Ainu Mosir* where the Ainu dwelled for a very long time. The new government also established the Hokkaido Colonialization Board and started to "develop" the land. This meant that the Ainu "lost" their homeland and were to become Japanese. Many hardships began to fall on the indigenous people.

The Colonization Board prohibited women's tattooing in 1871. The Ainu women had tattoos on their hands, wrists, and arms as well as around their mouths. Tattooing symbolized the adult women's beauty, and it had social and religious significance as the sign of a mature adult who can participate in weddings and rituals. It also gave the Ainu women an ethnic identity and pride. The Board banned men's earrings and encouraged the Ainu to learn oral and written Japanese language[145].

Mr. Nabesawa is interested in ecology, especially preserving the rich natural environment that surrounds his town. He said, "In those days there were wolves everywhere in Hokkaido before the colonization and land cultivation started. Wolves lived in groups and used to attack calves. Japanese colonialists killed so many wolves with guns and eliminated them. *Ezo ōkami* (wolves native to Hokkaido) thus became extinct. The Ainu lived in harmony with nature, including wolves. They were a hunting people, but they also grew grains, by the way. They knew the wolves' habits very well. When the Ainu went hunting, the wolves would howl and let the Ainu know that a bear was near or there was a group of deer. They transmitted the information to the Ainu hunters by the way they howled. It was a signal. The *Wajin* considered that wolves were bad guys that attacked farmers' livestock including calves and ponies, and thus the wolves interfered with their profit making. However, to the Ainu, the wolves were good guys who could help them with hunting. The Ainu and the wolves were in a symbiotic relationship." Mr. Nabesawa lamented that the natural environment that enabled the Ainu's unique way of life rapidly decayed when the ethnic majority Japanese settled in Hokkaido. Their ignorant over-harvesting of both meat and vegetables made food scarce.

"The *Wajin* did not understand ecology. Take deer hunting. The Ainu hunt mainly deer, not doe. If you keep hunting doe recklessly, we will starve one day. The same thing with fishing. We rarely catch salmon that are ready to lay eggs. It will lead to fewer salmon. Occasionally, we caught a salmon and ate its eggs though. The *Wajin* came over to Hokkaido, prohibited the Ainu from hunting deer and catching salmon in the river, and forced us to engage in farming. It was a total transformation of life style for the Ainu. The *Wajin* were more interested in agricultural business – making money.

"You know, the Ainu were a hunting people, but nutritionally, their diet was well-balanced. For example, there were plenty of mountain vegetables in the springtime. In autumn, salmon came up the rivers in tremendous numbers. The Ainu believe that gods exist in everything in the universe. Various gods descend to the human world to bring them food and furs. In May and June, the mountain dove gods let the Ainu know saying, 'Cultivate the field! Cultivate the field! Spring is here!' It's time to sow. Autumn is the time to harvest and enjoy a great meal. Women get together and cook, and they let the small children eat to their heart's content," Mr. Nabesawa said reminiscing about the good old days when the people lived more in tune with nature.

Mr. Nabesawa has been working as a farmer, and he grows rice and different kinds of vegetables such as cabbages, broccolis, cucumbers, eggplants, and so on. He has several greenhouses and all the mechanical equipment for his agricultural business. A few years ago, the town officials asked him to engage in a project of restoring *iwor*[146] (traditional Ainu living spaces). Mr. Nabesawa recreated a traditional vegetable garden on a riverbank near his house, and he has been very successful. He said, "My grandmother and I used to grow particular kinds of vegetables and grains, and my memories helped me a lot with the town's project."

[145] Kato & Wakazono. 2018, pp.64-69.

[146] www.bunka.go.jp/english/policy/cultural_properties/ainu. Accessed 4/14/19.

Figure 78 Inside one of Mr. Nabesawa's greenhouses.

Mr. Nabesawa also showed me several plants for religious ceremonies. He also showed me his saplings that he was ready to transplant. He then told me about a particular plant. He said, "The roots of *ikema* have poisons that are applied to arrows to kill animals. People also make charms with them to prevent catching an epidemic disease and avoid evils. You can wear the charm on your neck. The roots are also used as medicine for stomach ache and diarrhea by chewing a small amount of raw *ikema.*"

Figure 79 Mr. Nabesawa is showing me his saplings. He is going to transplant them soon.

Mr. Nabesawa has also been very active in his efforts to preserve their oral tradition. He said, "My wife said to me repeatedly, 'You start speaking in Ainu when you are drunk, and you know a lot about the Ainu. Why don't you contribute to the preservation of Ainu culture instead of just talking about these at home and only with your friends?' I want to thank my wife for motivating me. I now serve on several organizations as president and board member. I participate in Ainu cultural festivals and talent competitions. I regularly lecture to large groups of students and adults who visit the museums in town. I share my life stories and teach the history of the Ainu in the auditorium." These activities keep Mr. Nabesawa quite busy, but he really loves sharing stories about the Ainu people, history, and culture in public. He won a cultural award in a competition, and he was invited to perform *Yukar*, an epic poem in the form of verse, and received the award in the Tokyo's Ainu Cultural Festival several years ago. His wife said, "It was such a special occasion for celebration. The auditorium was full of people, and my husband performed *Yukar* to his heart's content. Our children also attended it, and they were very proud of their father. It really made both of us very happy."

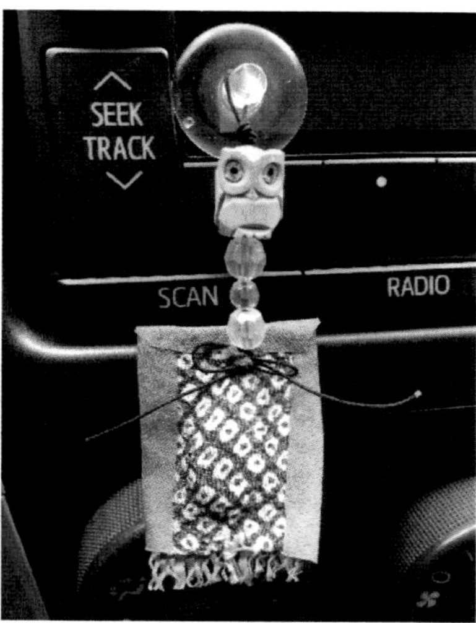

Figure 80 A protective charm with a hand-carved owl, beads, and the bag that contains roots of *ikema.* The Ainu believe the plant expels evil and bad luck.

Figure 81 Mr. Nabesawa is lecturing high school students from Honshu in an auditorium wearing full Ainu regalia, including a headdress. The black and white photo behind Mr. Nabesawa shows his grandmother kneeling in the far left and his grandfather standing in the far right next to the bear.

In June 2012, Mr. Nabesawa gave me a beautiful handmade stick called *repni* at the end of my stay at his house. The wooden stick is 13.5 inches long and has a small piece of deer horn with a string at one end. He told me that a talented Ainu storyteller performs *Yukar* by beating it against the wooden frame of a fireplace to keep rhythm.

"I made this, and I am giving it to you as my farewell gift," Mr. Nabesawa said handing it to me.

"Thank you so much! I really like it," I said as I received it.

"Dr. Kinko, you might need this to tell your story one day," Mr. Nabesawa said smiling.

It was a very nice heartfelt gift. I did not know why he chose the particular Ainu item as a gift to me at that time, but as I look back, it was a very appropriate gift since I am now writing his story.

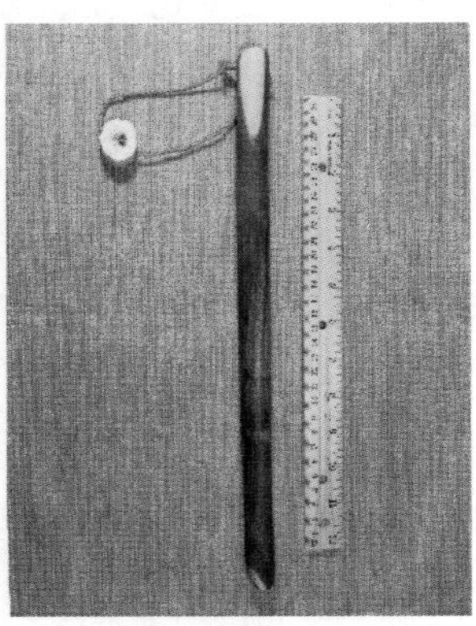

Figure 32 *Repni*, a handmade farewell gift Mr. Nabesawa gave me at the end of my stay at his house in 2012. The stick is for a storyteller to keep rhythm with when performing a *Yukar*.

In the summer of 2014, I obtained a $4,000 summer scholarship from the Dean's Office at my university to go back to Hokkaido, interview my Ainu informants, and shoot video clips as they talk about their experiences. My project entailed making multimedia archives of the elderly Ainu men and women's narratives as well as producing a feature-length documentary film. Videotaping would allow me to record their non-verbal communicational information, which is a very important and crucial aspect of high-context culture. In Japan, people depend more on gestures, facial expressions, tone of voice, grunts, eye contact, and length and timing of silence for cues for proper social interaction. The message is not only in words but also in the contexts. I would document their way of life in 21st century Japan – what they do, think, and feel now as well as their stories of their childhood and youth. I went back to Hokkaido and visited my Ainu informants including the Nabesawas again. They welcomed me so warmly once again and became my very gracious hosts.

Mr. Nabesawa took me around town in his Toyota, and showed me the places that are important to the Ainu. Some places were of historical, cultural, and social significance, and others were of ecological or linguistic significance. We visited Soma Shrine, one of the Shinto shrines in town, one day. Mr. Nabesawa said that there used to be many cherry trees at this shrine. The beautiful cherry blossoms are simply beautiful and gorgeous, and the Japanese traditionally love and cherish them. They are often associated with new beginnings since Japanese school starts when they are in full bloom in April. Cherry blossoms also remind the Japanese of the fleeting moments of life when the blossoms start to drop to the ground blown in the wind or rain.

Sitting on the steps of the entrance of the Shrine building, Mr. Nabesawa told me about an event during WWII when he and others in the community sent their young Ainu men to war. They praised the newly recruited soldiers, wished them luck, and cheered them by saying "*Banzai!*" (Long Live the Emperor!) They raised both hands three times, as they shouted. War was not a celebration at all, but that was how the soldiers went to war. Many Ainu men did not come back to Hokkaido. He looked very sad when he told me about the soldiers. Mr. Nabesawa said, "Japan was becoming a militaristic society at the time. The Great Military Headquarters (HQ) reported many victories. There were derogatory slogans used against the British or the United States. The HQ constantly reported on how many enemy airplanes and ships the Japanese military destroyed. The Japanese were brainwashed and believed their stories. Nevertheless, Japan was already heading for her defeat in 1944.

"We gathered here to pray for victory, and our elders performed *peotanke* to win the war. The *peotanke* ritual is to warn of a crisis, and women perform the crying. Moreover, the male elders raise their swords into the air a few times and chant in Ainu. It doesn't happen every day, and that is why I still remember it after 60, 70 years, just like yesterday," Mr. Nabesawa said.

"Were there many Ainu men who went to war?" I asked him.

"Well, we talk about discrimination and other things, but the Ainu men were drafted and sent to war just like everyone else. In those days the Ainu went to war, but they never became officers," he replied.

"Was it due to discrimination?" I asked.

"Perhaps. The Ainu men were less educated. Korean residents in Japan were classified not as soldiers but civilian employees. At least they called the Ainu soldiers, like the second or the third class soldiers. I think America is a much more democratic country. I am not quite sure since I lack knowledge, but I heard that in the American army, it was usually African-Americans who were sent to the battlefront first. Likewise, the Ainu went to the battlefields. They never became officers. I heard that they were also the first men sent to the battlefront," Mr. Nabesawa said.

I asked him how he felt about world peace. He said, "I want to advocate the idea that all the people around the world should become friends. This is the core of the Ainu spirituality, our group consciousness. We need to talk with one another. We may not be families or relatives, but when we communicate, we often find that we think alike. You are my brother, my friend. The Ainu have had this tradition for a very long time."

"How can we understand each other and become friends?" I asked Mr. Nabesawa.

"It's hard to answer. The United Nations declared Article 46. It declares all-inclusive human rights and covers all humans, humans all over the world. The Ainu call the earth where humans inhabit *Urespa Mosir*. It refers to the natural world itself where all living beings help each other grow and live together in symbiotic relations with nature. *Urespa* means that we mutually help each other grow. We need to understand that from now on," he said. The General Assembly adopted the United Nations Declaration on the Rights of Indigenous People on September 13, 2007. Mr. Nabesawa said, "Article 46 says, '... human rights and fundamental freedom of all shall be respected.'[147] You need to remember that it includes all people." Mr. Nabesawa also said, "We can communicate with our hearts. It has been my goal that I suggest people to communicate from their hearts with the people around the world and to recognize we are all humans and brothers. The earth where we all live is *Urespa Mosir* after all."

When I visited him in 2014, Mr. Nabesawa told me that he had been thinking about joining a class that teaches Esperanto, an artificial international language invented by a Polish man named L.L. Zamenhof[148]. He said, "I do not like nations asserting their rights and their national interests only. If everyone gets interested in the universal language, and speak it, I think it might contribute to the prevention of conflicts in the world. I've been thinking this way for a long time. We need to speak the same language that transcends vested interests in order to prevent religious conflicts, for example."

The Ainu word *caranke* refers to a debate to settle arguments and disputes. The *ukocaranke* refers to a discussion where everyone participates equally, and mutually share their opinions, ideas, and thoughts. It is a peaceful means to solve conflicts in an Ainu community. *Caranke* lasts for hours and days until the debaters reach reconciliation. The Chiefs of the

---

[147] www.iwgia.org/images/documenta/popular-publications/UNDRIP.pdf. Accessed 3/9/19.

[148] www.merriam-webster.com/dictionary/Esperanto. Accessed 4/14/19.

villages needed to be very good at reasoning and oratory. They also needed to have a tremendous amount of physical stamina.[149]

I asked Mr. Nabesawa for any suggestions for the young to cope with the problems they are facing today. He said, "I want to advise them to have confidence in themselves. They must do the things they should, whole-heartedly. They do not need to hide their Ainu ancestry or identity. Instead of following others, they need to take initiative, be creative, and do their best."

At the end of my stay in town in 2014, Mr. Nabesawa insisted that he perform an Ainu ritual of praying for my safe trip, as I was to depart to the United States soon. Mrs. Nabesawa and her friends also joined us. Mrs. Nabesawa had dressed me in traditional Ainu clothing at her house, and she had put a *matamps*, a headband with traditional Ainu embroidery, on my head as well. We went to a certain location for the sacred Ainu ritual, and I shot video clips for my documentary films.

Figure 83 Mr. Nabesawa is praying for me to have a safe journey back to the United States.

Mr. Nabesawa prayed to the Ainu God of Earth, first in the Ainu language, and then he explained what he said in Japanese. He said, "To the God of the Earth, I am going to give you prayers along with my friends according to our tradition. There is a big mountain named Porosiri near here, and I am an Ainu who lives in the downstream of the Saru River. All of us will make an offering to you and pray here at the foot of Yukkucikausi. A woman is going to take a very, very long journey across the ocean. God, please protect her on her journey." Mr. Nabesawa addressed the particular god who is the receiver of his prayers, first. He then identified himself and told the specific contents of his prayer. He offered *sake* to him with an *ikupasuy*, a thin wooden spatula that is about a foot long and used for offering *sake* to gods. He then said "thank you" as he opened his hands and raised both of his palms upward toward his face.

I dipped the *ikupasuy* (sacred spatula) into the *sake* in my bowl and offered *sake* to the god by splashing it over the fire. Then I moved the spatula over to my left shoulder, to my right shoulder, and then over my head splashing *sake*. I touched my left palm with my right index finger, and then I moved my finger from the left to right over my lips. I drank *sake* from the bowl with both of my hands and said, "Thank you." Actually, I pretended to drink *sake* since I do not drink alcohol at all. I had asked Mr. Nabesawa about it, and he said, "It's okay." When all the participants finished their offerings, Mr. Nabesawa finished the ritual by saying, "All of us have just finished making an offering to you at the foot of sacred Yukkucikausi. We offered our prayer."

149 Nobuyuki Ogasawara. 2004, p. 101. Yoichi Tsunoda. 2018, pp.202-203.

Figure 84 A bowl and *Ikupasuys* (sacred spatulas) with different designs for religious ceremonies (Photo by the author and courtesy of the Historical Museum of Saru River).

The shooting of the video clips went very well, and I left town for the United States. I kept in touch with Mr. Nebesawa by writing letters and calling him occasionally on the phone. In August 2017, I received an e-mail that Mr. Nabesawa's health had been deteriorating, and he was in a hospital. I called him at his house after I heard that he left the hospital.

"*Nabesawa Ekasi* (Elder Nabesawa)! It's me Kinko!" I greet him.

"Ohhhh, Dr. Kinko!!" Mr. Nabesawa says delightedly as usual, but I find his voice seems rather weak.

"I heard about your health. I hope you will get better soon," I say.

"Thank you! Now that I am talking to you, I feel getting better already!" Mr. Nabesawa says cheerfully. I remember him always being perky and happy when I was visiting him.

"Thank you so much for all the help with my filming! My documentary film has been very popular, and many people have seen it on YouTube!" I say.

"That's a great news!! I am very glad you called me. Are you in America now?" Mr. Nabesawa asks me.

"No, I am visiting my mother. I lost my father in 2015, and she is a widow," I say.

"Oh, I am very sorry, but I am sure your father was very proud of you," he says.

"Thank you," I say.

"Is there any chance you can come to Hokkaido? I want to see you again," he says.

"I'm sorry but not this time. But I promise I will come and see you next spring. I really want to see you, too!" I say.

"Well, I will be looking forward to seeing you again," he says.

"I will come at the beginning of May in 2018, okay? Actually, I am planning to have a lunch party for my Ainu friends in a restaurant right now. Of course, you are invited!!" I say.

"That's wonderful! I will see you then!" Mr. Nabesawa says.

I was very busy during the spring semester 2018 teaching and making another documentary film on the Ainu, a sequel to my previous one. I scheduled my flight to Tokyo on May 10 and another flight from Tokyo to Hokkaido on the following day. I started packing my suitcase in the middle of April for my trip since I needed my winter and spring clothes for Hokkaido up north and early summer clothes for Nagoya in central Japan. I sent invitations to all Ainu elder informants of mine for the luncheon that I was holding at a restaurant in their town. I was really looking forward to meeting them all. I really wanted to thank them for their contribution not only to my research projects but also for sharing their stories so that people around the world can get to know them and their life stories.

On May 1, I received an e-mail from Hideki, a museum staffer with whom Mr. Nabesawa was on very good terms. I think that they were actually very good friends. He said that Mr. Nabesawa had passed away on April 30, exactly two weeks before the luncheon that I organized for my Ainu informants and friends. I was shocked to hear the news and cried. Mr. Nabesawa was so generous with his time and taught me so many things as if he was my professor. I have been very sad about losing Mr. Nabesawa, but I am glad and thankful that I could stay at Mr. Nabesawa's house and interview him in 2012, and that he let me videotape him in 2014.

The luncheon on May 14, 2018 felt a bit funny without Mr. Nabesawa. Some elders talked about Mr. Nabesawa's virtues, talents, and contribution to transmitting the Ainu culture to the public over so many years. We all missed him so much. I had invited his wife to join us at the luncheon, but she could not come. She was in mourning, and she was supposed to avoid joyous social events or gatherings for a certain period after her husband's death. I sent her *gobutsuzen*, which is "a cash gift for the deceased." We missed the presence of Mr. and Mrs. Nabesawa at the luncheon, but we managed to have a very good time eating delicious food, talking, and joking together.

Figure 85 The luncheon with some of my Ainu informants on 5/14/2018.

Chapter 8: The Ainu Language

Mr. Tamotsu Nabesawa was one of the very few native speakers of Ainu. He lived with his grandmother who only spoke Ainu until his late teen years. He taught me a lot about the Ainu language. He also took me to various locations around town and explained to me the original meanings of the Ainu names. What is the Ainu language like?

The UNESCO classifies the Ainu language as critically endangered. It means that "the youngest speakers are grandparents and older, and they speak the language partially and infrequently."[150] The number of native speakers of Ainu has been dwindling due to the advanced age of the speakers. However, many young Ainu are taking lessons in Ainu at schools, universities, and community centers. Efforts in revitalization of the language have been taking place in recent years. For example, in 2018, Donan Bus Company that operates local bus service in Biratori Town started their bilingual announcements and information brochures in both Japanese and Ainu, regarding bus stops and schedules for their customers. The bus company also offers the same service for its express buses between its Hidaka Terminal and Sapporo Station Terminal and between Hidaka Terminal and Tomakomai Station.

The Ainu language used to be spoken not only in Hokkaido and in the northern part of Honshu but also in the southern half of Sakhalin and the Kuril Islands that are now occupied by Russia. It seems that there have been no speakers of Ainu in the Kuril Islands since the 1910s, and the majority of Ainu who lived in Sakhalin moved to Japan during World War II when it became a Russian territory. Today the Ainu speaking regions are limited to the Pacific coast and along the Ishikari River.[151]

Scholars consider that the Ainu language is an isolate language, and its origin and language family are not known. Ainu differs significantly from Japanese, and it is not a dialect of Japanese. For example, as compared with Japanese, Ainu always requires a subject (just like in English), and the verbs have singular and plural forms. Ainu does not have the present or past tense; adverbs or adverbial phrases such as "tomorrow" or "since then" give the temporal reference points. As far as word order is concerned, Ainu is very similar to that of Japanese. The Ainu did not have a system of writing, and they transmitted everything orally. Thus, it is very difficult to prove the relationship between the Japanese and Ainu languages due to the lack of historical and linguistic data.[152] Certain loan words exist between the two languages as well. Some of the Ainu words that are introduced to Japanese include *rakko* (sea otter), *tonakai* (reindeer), *shishamo* (capelin), *nonno* (flower), *hasukappu* (blue honeysuckle), and *etopirika* (tufted puffin).[153]

Ainu has many words that end with a consonant while the Japanese words always end with vowels except in the case of "n." In today's Japan, *katakana* characters and roman letters are commonly used in writing the Ainu language. Foreigners visiting Hokkaido in the late 1800s and early 1900s began writing down the Ainu language with their alphabets, namely Latin and Cyrillic characters. Some of them were scholars of East Asian Studies, social activists, missionaries, and medical doctors. Since the Meiji Period (1868 – 1912), scholars in cultural

---

[150] UNESCO Atlas of the World's Languages in Danger. www.unesco.org/new/en/culture/themes/endangered-languages/atlas-of-languages-in-danger. Accessed 4/10/19.
[151] Ainu Hakubutsukan. Pp.13-14.
[152] Ainu Minzoku Hakubutsukan 2009.
[153] Hideaki Uemura. 2008. P.103.

anthropology and linguistics tried to preserve the Ainu language by writing in Japanese. Some people such as Shigeru Kayano used the modern technology of tape recording and left many valuable audio tapes.[154]

Mr. Tamotsu Nabesawa, one of my main informants, was an *ekasi* (Ainu elder) who was bilingual in Ainu and Japanese. He was very active in preserving the Ainu culture and tradition. He said, "I think it is good to write the Ainu language in Japanese characters regarding the preservation of the words and their meanings. However, phonetically, the written Japanese words can be slightly different from the Ainu pronunciation." Written Japanese uses *hiragana* and *katakana* characters that are phonetic scripts (syllabaries). They are abbreviated versions of Chinese characters developed by the 10th century. The Japanese use *hiragana*, *katakana*, Chinese, and Roman characters in their everyday writing.[155]

Ainu has words that cannot be written in Japanese in exactly the same way as they are pronounced in Ainu. Each *hiragana* or *katakana* represents a sound made up of (1) vowels such as [u] and [o], (2) a consonant and a vowel as in [hi] and [ke], (3) contracted sounds made up of two consecutive consonants and a vowel such as [cha] and [kyo], and (4) an [n] sound. In addition to the normal sized *katakana,* smaller-sized version is used for recording certain sounds of the Ainu language. Roman letters such as p, t, k, m, and n, which appear at the end of a word, have been replaced by *katakana* letters in smaller size (ㇷ゚, ッ, ㇰ, ㇺ, ㇴ). The *katakana* scripts differ depending on the vowel sounds that are right before s, and r, which also appear at the end of certain words. However, when it comes to hearing, a Japanese might find it difficult to hear the difference between words such as *sap* (to go to a beach), *sat* (to dry), and *sak* (~ is lacking). The Ainu word *sap* is not pronounced in the same way as in English, and a listener often cannot distinguish whether the word she heard was *sap*, *sat*, or *sak.*[156] In 2000, JIS X 0213, computer language software, became available, and it made it possible for the Ainu language to be written more precisely.[157] JIS stands for Japanese Industrial Standard.

We must also remember that few ethnic groups developed their own letters. Most ethnic groups have adopted letters from another group and adapted them to their own language. The Japanese historians, administrators, and scholars used Chinese to write the Japanese language until the 9th and 10th centuries when the Japanese letters were developed. *Hiragana* and *katakana*, the new Japanese phonetic symbols were abbreviated and simplified versions of Chinese characters. Edwin Reischauer says that the Japanese system of writing "remains probably the most difficult and cumbersome in common use anywhere in the world[158]" and "The *kana* syllables also made possible more extensive literary works in Japanese.[159]"

The Ainu did not have letters, and this lack of a writing system makes it very difficult to prove the relationship between Japanese and Ainu languages. In order to study the history of the Ainu, the scholars also must depend on history written by the Japanese, whether they were administrators, explorers, or journalists. Thus, the Ainu history is a history recorded by outsiders whose values and culture were different, and it could contain mistakes or misunderstandings. Generally speaking, a history is usually written by the perspectives of the powerful. The history of the powerless is often lost and not represented in official history. For reconstruction of the

---

[154] Shigeru Kayano. 2009.
[155] Edwin O. Reischauer. 1990, pp.28-30.
[156] Ainu Minzoku Hakubutsukan. 2009, p.18.
[157] Hideaki Uemura. 2008, p.103.
[158] Edwin O. Reischauer. 1990, p.32.
[159] Edwin O. Reischauer. 1990, p.29.

Ainu history, it is necessary to evaluate the facts presented in orally transmitted histories and epics. In addition, archaeological and anthropological perspectives must be considered in order to reconstruct Ainu history.

The Ainu language also has regional differences, and there is no such thing as a standard Ainu language. Mrs. Sachiko Kibata told me about the experience of one of her students who went to Shizunai and met some Ainu people. She said, "Here, we say *Irankarapte*, which means 'Hello' and 'How are you?' In Shizunai and Urakawa, they say *Ikatay*. My student greeted them saying, '*Irankarapte*' because he wanted to be friendly. However, they greeted him back with *Ikatay*. He thought he heard *epatay*, which means 'stupid.' They confused him since he thought that they said, 'You are stupid.' He had tried to greet them in Ainu to be nice, but he felt mortified. Later, he learned that *Ikatay* means 'Hello' over there. He understood the regional difference and felt not too bad. But at first, he said he was mortified and felt uncomfortable."

Another example of regional differences are the names of their traditional clothing. The Ainu in the Hidaka region have worn *kaparamip* for formal and festive occasions since the Meiji Period (1868 – 1912). White cotton cloths are appliqued onto the black cotton kimono to make the traditional Ainu design on the front and back of the kimono. The Ainu call it *cikarkarpe* in the Shizunai region. *Cijiri* is another Ainu kimono. The women embroider their traditional design directly on the cotton kimono. The Ainu in the eastern part of Hokkaido call *cijiri cikarkarpe*.[160]

Figure 86 *Kaparamip* is called *cikarkarpe* in the Shizunai Region (Photo by the author: courtesy of the Historical Museum of Saru River).

The Ainu lived harmoniously in nature and never had a nation of their own, and this is possibly among the reasons why they did not develop a written language. A nation would need it in order to keep records of communication and taxes, as well as the history of a ruling tribe. The Ainu lacked powerful leaders and had no central government of their own.[161]

The Ainu have a very strong oral tradition that includes *Yukar* (a long epic about heroes) and *Uepeker* (traditional folk ballads), which enabled them to preserve history. They are masters of narration, and today they recite their world-famous *Yukar* at their cultural events. For example, *Kamuy yukar* tells stories of Ainu gods. The epic stories and poems, chants, lullabies, and traditional folk ballads were passed on from generation to generation around the fire at home or at the close of ancient festivals.[162]

---

[160] Yoichi Tsunoda. 2018, p. 149.

[161] Ainu Minzoku Hakubutsukan. 2009, p.22.

Figure 87 An Ainu woman is embroidering traditional designs onto blue fabric, which is appliqued to the bottom layer made of *attus* (fabric made of tree fiber).

Traditionally, oratory was highly praised by the Ainu, and thus, oratorical skills gave the Ainu social power. Oratory was one of the requirements for becoming a leader because the Ainu believed that words have great power that can heal or kill. They engaged in peaceful debates called *ukocaranke* that lasted for days in order to settle matters, a feat that required both physical stamina and speaking skills.[163]

The assimilation policy of the Japanese government contributed to the loss of the Ainu language in everyday usage. Mr. Nabesawa said, "Until the *Wajin* advanced to Hokkaido, the Ainu were speaking their own language, and most of them could not speak Japanese. When contacts with *Wajin* increased, a situation arose in which the Ainu had to speak Japanese. The language acquisition became a necessity for survival. Of course, there were no problems when the Ainu were speaking to other Ainu people. The Japanese administration did not want the Ainu to speak their language because their inability to understand Ainu would cause problems in dealing with them. At the same time, there were *Wajin* merchants who got very good at speaking the Ainu language and learned the Ainu culture in order to benefit from trading with them."

Mr. Nabesawa also said, "To the Ainu people, the term 'Ainu' which means 'humans' came to have a discriminatory, negative, and derogatory connotation due to prejudice, discrimination, bullying, and other social problems." Interestingly, the Ainu avoided the word themselves at one point. For example, Hokkaido Ainu Association established in 1946 is the largest organization of the Ainu people. It changed its name to the Hokkaido *Utari* Association in April 1961. *Utari* means "fellows, brothers, and comrades." Then, as the Ainu started to increase their ethnic awareness and identity, they realized that the original meaning of the word is very positive. They switched the name of the association back to the Hokkaido Ainu Association in April 2009.

Many of the Ainu population used to hide their identities in order to avoid prejudice and discrimination in employment, education, and marriage. They consciously avoided speaking in the Ainu language. These social problems must be resolved if the Ainu people are to feel free to communicate in their own language. Mr. Kawanano and Mrs. Kibata told me in my interview that when they were young their parents told them that they did not have to speak Ainu even at home, not to mention at school because of bullying and teasing by the *Wajin* children. Thus, their

[162] Yoichi Tsunoda. 2018, pp.182-185.

[163] Shigeru Kayano. 2009.

parents thought their children did not need to learn the language. Mr. Kawanano and Mrs. Kibata said in my interview that they still vividly remember their grandparents speaking the Ainu among themselves.[164]

Many Ainu words and Japanese words that derive from the Ainu language appear as place names in Hokkaido and the northern part of Honshu. These names describe geographic and topographic features such as Shikotsu ("big-hollow"), Wakkanai ("cold-drinking-water-river/swamp"), Sapporo (possibly "a dry-vast-place"), and Rishiri ("a high mountain"). The words used to be an important source of information for the hunting and fishing Ainu. Kayano (2009) states that the ubiquitous names of places that are in the Ainu language in Hokkaido prove that it was indeed the homeland of the Ainu, and the Japanese unlawfully invaded it, oppressed, and exploited the Ainu.

The Japanese government recognized the traditional Ainu dancing as an important intangible folk cultural asset in 1984. It gave the Ainu pride and esteem in their ethnicity. Since then, the Ainu have come to realize that their language is also indispensable to their cultural consciousness. Many Ainu language classes have been offered since 1987, especially in cities and towns in Hokkaido. By 1993, there were 11 Ainu language classes offered in Biratori, Asahikawa, Sapporo, Kushiro, Uraga, Shiraoi, Chitose, Shizunai, Mukawa, Akan, and Obihiro, and textbooks have been written for those students of the Ainu language. Institutions of higher education, including Hokkaido University of Education in Sapporo, Hokkai Gakuen University, and Sapporo Gakuin University, have developed special academic curricula for teaching the Ainu language and culture. Universities and museums offer lectures on the Ainu language and culture. Once considered a vanishing language, Ainu is currently reviving in academia and local communities.

GOLDEN KAMUY, a very popular Japanese manga series and anime, has added fuel to the interests in the Ainu language since 2014. It is the first bilingual manga/animation in Japanese and Ainu languages. Now the mass media contributes to the revival of the critically endangered language. The comic story also teaches the readers and audience Ainu words along with idioms, proverbs, customs and manners, Ainu history, cuisine, religions, and traditional life.

The UNESCO Atlas of the World's Languages in Danger states that the youngest speakers of a critically endangered language are "grandparents and older, and they speak the language partially and infrequently."[165] *Asirpa*, her grandmother, and other Ainu speak freely in their mother tongue in the comic story and in the anime version. In a sense, *GOLDEN KAMUY* is the very first bilingual comic in Japanese and Ainu languages. Even though the Ainu is an isolate language and the readers and audience are not familiar with it at all, they repeatedly learn the words, sounds, and meanings. They start to master Ainu words such as those of animals (brown bears, deer, squirrels, etc.), birds (both native and migrant), plants (vegetables, mountain vegetables, and other plants), fish (in rivers and sea), traditional Ainu dishes, and gods as well as adjectives such as delicious and beautiful. The readers and audience also learn Ainu proverbs, idioms, and greetings in certain episodes. One of the Ainu words that is very popular with the young readers is *osoma* (poop). The word appears quite often and usually in a comparison with *miso* (fermented soybean paste). For example, Sugimoto loves putting *miso* into his soup and other dishes, and *Asirpa* often teases him that he is eating poop. Obviously, the Ainu at that time did not know of the bean paste. *Hinna* is a word of gratitude, and the Ainu use the word to mean

---

[164] Kazunobu Kawanano and Sachiko Kibata. 2015. *Have You Heard about the Ainu?*

[165] www.unesco.org/new/en/culture/themes/endangered-languages/atlas-of-languages-in-danger/ Accessed 4/15/19.

"delicious." The words *osoma* and *hinna* occasionally appear together in the scenes where Sugimoto and *Asirpa* are eating, and Noda portrays *Asirpa* in such a comical way that the readers and audience delight in her various facial expressions.

Other Ainu words that appear in *GOLDEN KAMUY* includes *asir* (new), *saranip* (a woven carrying bag), *yukker* (shoes made of deerskin), *kuca* (temporary hut), *citatap* (a dish with ground meat), *ohaw* (soup), *pu* (food storage), *ekasi* (Ainu elder/grandfather), *wakka* (water), *retar* (white), *ruype* (thawed frozen salmon), *cip* (a boat), just to name a few. These words introduced in the comic story become a living language among readers. A language follows the principle of "use it or lose it." Thus, people's usage helps the language live and prevents it from becoming extinct. *GOLDEN KAMUY* is a *manga* that has a linguistic significance in this sense. Just like Americans use certain Japanese words such as *sushi*, *sashimi*, *tataki*, *kaizen*, *bonsai*, *haiku*, *karaoke*, *hibachi*, *sumo*, and *futon* in their everyday life, the Ainu words become a living vocabulary and we can avoid extinction.

Ernesto Ottone Ramirez, a UNESCO Assistant Director-General for Culture, commented, "Indigenous languages are reservoirs of meaning, knowledge, culture, and identities."[166] The Ainu language has rarely appeared in the Japanese mass media, but now *GOLDEN KAMUY* is revitalizing the critically endangered language. The revitalization can lead to a revival of the language when many young people in the world start to understand the Ainu language.

---

[166] www.unesco.org/new/en/unesco-liaison-office-in-new-york/about-this-office/single-view/news/lauunch_of_the_2019_international_year_of_indigenous_languages
Accessed 4/15/19.

Chapter 9: The Ainu Religion

Monotheistic religions have only one Deity, for example, God Almighty in Christianity, Allah in Islam, and Yahweh in Judaism. The Ainu religion is animistic and polytheistic just like Shinto, the indigenous Japanese religion that worships 8 million *kami*s (gods). Shinto, or "the way of the gods." Shinto is Japan's indigenous and animistic religion that revolves around the objects, phenomena, and events that pertain to nature. It follows the principle of co-existence with nature. In Shinto, there are *yao yorozu no kami* (8 million gods). The Ainu consider that there are spirits, or life forces everywhere. For example, we can find the spirits in mountains, bears, foxes, plants, fish, water, fire, natural disasters, wind, earthquakes, boats, dishes, houses, and even toilets! They all descend from Heaven with a mission, live on earth in many different forms, and they are all equal in having previous lives. The spirits here are living things with life force. For the Ainu, various gods are in charge of certain functions on earth, both naturalistic and materialistic. There are gods with strong spirits in fire, tsunamis, thunder, mortars, and pestles. Important gods include *shima* owl, wolves, bears, foxes, Hokkaido squirrels, whales, swordfish, turtles, and salmon. What the Ainu recognize as gods are those that are necessary and beneficial to human life, and they have very strong spirits that humans cannot manipulate. They seem to have human like emotions. Those who threaten human life are bad gods.[167]

Figure 88 A carved Blakiston's fish owl at the roadside. The Ainu call it *kotankorkamuy*, a god that owns the village. It is also a god of hunting and protection.

The Ainu live in harmony with nature and have never hunted or harvested too much. They take from nature according to what they need. In this sense, they lead an eco-friendly life in a symbiotic relationship with nature. For the Ainu, the roles of god spirits and humans exist in a perfect harmony with nature as a medium. In religious rituals, the Ainu "seek to please the good spirits and prevent evil ones from causing sickness and misfortune."[168] Good gods are benefactors to human life while evil ones threaten humans. The Ainu traditionally practiced exorcism to drive away wicked spirits. At two of my informants' stores, I purchased several Ainu good luck charms that have dried plants and talisman as souvenir gifts for me and my friends. They are supposed to protect us from evil and bring us good luck.

---

[167] Yoichi Tsunoda. 2018.

[168] Mary Ine Hilger. 1967, p.271.

Figure 89 Nusa, an Ainu religious alter with *inaws* (shaved wood sticks given to gods as gifts).

The Ainu call the world we live in Ainu *Mosir* (human country), and as for the next world, they have two concepts. There are regional differences among them, and the next world could be in heaven or underground. There is an entrance to the next world called "the-other-world-entering-road-entrance" or "go-road-entrance."[169] The sceneries and environments are supposed to be almost the same whether in heaven or underground. The deceased leave this world with articles buried in a tomb after a funeral. The spirit goes through the entrance, and it is born again. The next world is exactly the same kind of land as on earth, and it is where the deceased's ancestors are waiting. The newly deceased thus must bring as many souvenirs as possible to them, and they would welcome the tokens wholeheartedly. They bury the dead body since it does not have a soul. The person now lives among the ancestors and friends and is remembered when the Ainu drink and eat together. The Ainu practice of visiting graveyards was not a custom until the Japanese immigrated to Hokkaido. The *Wajin* had Japanese-style (Buddhist) funerals there, and they introduced the custom of visiting graveyards on the day when the dead souls return to the earth in the middle of August.

When an Ainu dies, they dispatch the spirit of the deceased by burning the mementos and the deceased's empty house. The Japanese government prohibited this custom, as well as the tattooing of women and pierced earrings of men in 1871.

One of the most well-known religious rites of the Ainu is called *iyomante*, which literally means, "Let the god (= bear) go."[170] It is a ritual to send back the spirit of the bear to its ancestors in the god's country. The Ainu traditionally believed that a god in the form of a bear comes to visit humans and provides them with meat and fur. The bear is thus a god of food, and the Ainu calls it *kimunkamuy* ("the mountain god"). The god wears a great black kimono and lives in *Kamuy Mosir* (Gods' land) like a human being does. When he misses *sake* and *inaw*, he comes down to the *Ainu Mosir* (Human Land) disguising himself as a bear and brings meat, fur, and an organ that the humans use as a medicine.[171]

[169] Ainu Minzoku Hakubutsukan. 2009, pp.151-152.
[170] Ainu Minzoku Hakubutsukan. 2009, p.159.
[171] Yoichi Tsunoda. 2018, p.48.

Figure 90 Inaws (shaved wooden sticks) and food offerings at the *nusa* (religious altar).

The *iyomante* ritual entails hunting a hibernating bear between the beginning of winter and early spring. The Ainu send the spirit of an adult bear back to the god's country right on the hunting ground while its meat and fur are brought back to the community. The Ainu honors the bear and have a big festival. The Ainu might find a cub, which was born in January or February, in the same cave. The Ainu will bring it back to the community, where it will be kept in a cage made of wooden bars, and taken good care of for a few years. The cub is now more than 200 pounds and will pose a danger to humans if it keeps growing. The owner of the bear plans an *iyomante* ceremony during the month of February. He sends messengers to a nearby village to announce the event and invite the villagers.

Not only the people in the *kotan* (Ainu community) but also many guests came to the ceremony and reception from faraway places. The preparation took a lot of time and effort, and the people divided major tasks among themselves. The ritual of *iyomante* includes the sacrifice of the bear. The Ainu bombards it with blunt arrows at the festival. They send the spirit of the *kimunkamuy* to the gods' country where its mother is.

The Ainu people gather and give much food, liquor, swords, and other treasures to the bear as souvenir gifts. They also recite *Yukar*, chant prayers for the spirit to come back to earth and bless them, dance, and feast all night. Interestingly, the singer stops his *Yukar* half way when the story becomes very exciting. This is to make the *kimunkamuy* want to come back to the village to listen to the rest of the epic poem.

The Ainu did not have any notion of killing the bear. *Iyomante* honors the spirit and shows the Ainu's appreciation for the creature and its visit. The spirit, after it leaves the body, is invited and welcomed in the community or in a house as a guest. The spirit is also entertained when the Ainu wine and dine with it. The Ainu take care of the cranium of the bear with respect, adorn it with *inaw* sacred wood shavings, and leave it on their religious alter outside of the house. Japanese government prohibited the spiritual ceremony for its cruelty, and made it illegal in 1872.[172]

I mentioned the wooden bears that an Ainu artisan carved, which my father purchased. The bears became exceptionally popular as one of the best souvenirs from Hokkaido between the middle of the 1960s to the middle of the 1970s. So did the wooden pair of an Ainu couple in their traditional clothes with a headdress (husband) and a headband (wife). However, the Ainu did not engage in idol worship, or idol production until the end of the Taisho Period (1912-1926). The Ainu considered all animals as divine benefactors to the humans. They thought that

[172] Ainu Hakubutsukan. 2009, pp.159-162. Yoichi Tsunoda. 2018, pp.166-167. Shigeru Kayano. 2007, pp. 31-40.

producing an item using the gods' images was a disrespectful action toward the gods and were afraid of retaliation and negative sanctions. The Ainu traditionally excelled in woodcarving as they made knives, trays, sacred spatulas, and cigarette cases with Ainu designs.[173]

[173] FRPAC. 2012, pp.10-11.

Chapter 10: The Story of "Lily" – My first Ainu friend

Mr. Kawanano became my "Ainu father" in 2011, and he has been helping me achieve my research goals since then. One of the best things he did for me was to introduce Hideki whom he knew through his volunteer work. Hideki worked as a staff member at one of the museums in town for many years. Several years after my visits, he received a promotion and transferred to another section of the town hall. He is very friendly and has a nice personality. He is several years younger than I am, but we have the same kind of experiences and memories as cotemporary cohorts. He promised Mr. Kawanano that he would support my research agenda, and he became my main *Wajin* informant. I told him that I wanted to meet many people, both Ainu and *Wajin*, during my short visit in 2011. Hideki introduced his friends and acquaintances, both Ainu and *Wajin*, worked on my interview schedule in 2012, and he gave me rides to the various places along with other Ainu informants. I met "Lily" through Hideki during my first visit in 2011. The people he introduced to me in turn introduced their family members, friends, and acquaintances. Sociologists and statisticians call it "snowball sampling.[174]"

"Let me introduce you to Lily. She is an Ainu woman with whom I used to work in various archaeological excavation sites in town some years ago. She is diligent and pays attention to minute details. She was one of the best diggers ever. I contacted her already and told about you. She is coming to the museum this afternoon," Hideki says.

"Wow! That is great! Thank you so much," I say to him.

"You are going to like her," he says and smiles.

Lily came to the museum, and Hideki introduced us. An older woman staff member served us green tea, and the three of us talked in the staff room. Lily seemed to be a bit shy at first, but she quickly got used to me, a researcher from America who was interested in studying the Ainu people. This was my first time meeting her, but it seemed like I had already known her from somewhere. I am sure some of my readers have had the same kind of experience that gives them a strong feeling of familiarity. As I kept talking with her, I found myself liking her. I felt like I was really supposed to meet her.

Lily was very curious about the everyday life in the United States and seemed to like hearing about my experiences and life philosophy. We shared the same kind of sense of humor and sarcasm, too. I truly have benefitted from our friendship and her generosity to share her life experiences as an Ainu woman.

Here is Lily's story.

"My father was born in Honshu and came to this town as a backpacker in the late 1960s. He stayed in a place where backpackers flocked in those days. He loved Hokkaido, found a job, and married my mother, who is an Ainu. So, I am a so-called 'half.'

"I met Kimura, my future husband, when I was 20 or 21. He was born in Tokyo and was four years older than I was. Many Japanese tourists flocked to our town in the late 1980s and right after the Heisei Period (1989 – 2019) started. Many of the young men from Honshu would stay in prefabricated houses here for months or years. They could have run away from the hustle and bustle of the city life, or they might have just loved the slow and nice rural life in Hokkaido.

---

[174] www.statisticshowto.datasciencecentral.com/snowball-sampling. Accessed 2/23/19.

"My Ainu friend knew Kimura, and she introduced me to him. At that time, I was in love with an older man. It was platonic love, but I felt very comfortable and content when I was with him. I do not think he was interested in me as a woman because of the age difference.

"I left home and lived in a town in Hokkaido, which is well-known for its hot springs. I worked in a souvenir shop, which was seasonal work. I was there only from May to the end of October. I did not work the rest of the year and got unemployment benefits. Sometimes I worked in an excavation site. I love digging, and I am very interested in what we find there, like pieces of pottery from the ancient times. You put together a pottery object from all these pieces as if it is a jigsaw puzzle. The beautiful designs these ancient people made with ropes still fascinate me.

"I returned home to my parents' house when the tourist season was over, and I stopped by at my girlfriend's house one day. Kimura was there along with some other *Wajin* men from Honshu. I think he fell in love with me. He wanted to have a date, but to me, it was like 'Who the heck is this guy?' That was my first impression of him. I declined the offer right away. However, when he called me to have a date with me when I was in the spa town later, I decided to give him a chance. We went to Otaru and did some sightseeing. That was the beginning of our relationship.

"Kimura's parents were opposed to our marriage because he is a *Wajin*, and I am an Ainu. My parents did not oppose it even though they had some reservations. My Ainu mother warned me saying, 'There are few marriages that go very well. You will have a difficult time.' I married Kimura after a certain period of engagement.

"I did not want to leave Hokkaido by all means, and I made Kimura promise me that we would not leave here for whatever reason. I had been enjoying our honeymoon period when Kimura got a job near Tokyo for six months. I was not particularly excited about living in an urban area. Tokyo never sleeps. Wherever you go, it is always crowded. People, people, people! It's noisy all the time. The air is not clean. Criminal incidents take place such as pickpockets, thefts, and murders. At night, there are no stars!

"But the big city did have advantages. There are so many people in Tokyo, and nobody knew that I was an Ainu. I can easily blend in with other Japanese or foreigners, and nobody notices me there. In a small rural town, I always have to watch out what I say and do because people know that I am an Ainu. I always try to do my best.

"When my husband and I returned to Hokkaido, I locked all the doors at night and when I went out. My neighbors asked me, 'Why do you need to lock your house?' I had gotten so used to the way of urban life I forgot how safe and nice my hometown really was.

"We had two children. When Kimura's uncle wanted him to work in his company, my husband decided to leave Hokkaido again. The company was located in a city in Niigata prefecture. I pleaded with him not to accept the job offer, but he did. I was reluctant to go there, but Kimura convinced me that he would love and protect me as always.

"We moved to a town in Niigata. Soon after we arrived, his aunt said to me, 'Don't tell anyone that you are an Ainu.' Hokkaido was getting much attention in those days, and the mass media featured its tourism very often. I wondered why Kimura's aunt had to say such a thing to me. Then I remembered that my husband's parents were opposed to their son's marrying an Ainu.

"As my mother warned, I did have a hard time with his relatives in Honshu. They were different from the kind of people I am used to here in Hokkaido. They have very strong prejudice against the Ainu. Even when they were nice to me, which was seldom, I could not trust them wholeheartedly. My husband's aunt was a control freak, and she would pick out an apartment for us as well as a kindergarten for our kids. She wanted to decide many things for us.

"We moved to a new apartment. It had two stories, and there were six units. I got a phone call from a stranger one day. He said to me, 'Let's go to a hotel.' I thought that was a prank call and simply said, 'You have a wrong number. The next time you call me, I'll call the police.' The next day, someone rang our bell. When I went to the door, I found nobody. The culprit turned out to be our neighbor. He was upset that we left our bicycles, my kids' bikes, and mine right outside of our apartment. He got our phone number from the realtor. He also talked about us to his wife and children in a negative manner.

"One time I suffered from high fever and went to a hospital. I was diagnosed with acute pneumonia. My relatives picked up my two children and took care of them while I was recuperating in the hospital. When I was leaving the hospital, they said to me coldly, 'Don't you ever get sick again!' I missed my Mom and my family very much. I really wanted to go back to Hokkaido.

"I was homesick and called home every day. My mother sent me sweets made in Hokkaido once a week to soothe me. My mother-in-law told me, 'Don't call Hokkaido every day. It costs a lot of money.' Luckily, I soon had a chance to go back home to visit my parents for a short while. I purchased a few boxes of very expensive brand-name chocolates made in Hokkaido. They were not easily available in Honshu in those days. I brought them back to Kimura's relatives. Those who received the chocolates were very happy, but the others who learned that they did not get one blamed me as unfair. They said, 'Why didn't you buy a box for us?'

"You know, Hokkaido was once a frontier, and the ancestors of the people who live here now came from different parts of Japan. Thus, I think the customs and manners are more flexible, and there is lots of leeway regarding what we should do, say, for wedding ceremonies, receptions, and gifts. Many people in Hokkaido might opt for not having the expensive engagement ceremony where the two families exchange gifts before their wedding. Instead, they might have a wedding ceremony and reception where everyone pays the same amount of money as 'a participation fee' instead of *oshūgi* cash gift. I heard that the rate for *oshūgi* is like at least 10,000 yen (@US$90), and some bring like 30,000 yen, or even 50,000 yen. That is a lot of money out of your pocket just to attend the wedding reception. We are less formal, and there is more freedom here in Hokkaido. I married a *Wajin* from Tokyo, and we had an engagement ceremony. I did not like some of the formalities regarding customs and manners in Honshu. There are also adults who would bully other adults. Some people are cold.

"When my desire to go back home to Hokkaido was reaching its peak, Kimura's cousin invited me to a bar-restaurant to discuss matters with me. It was an establishment where a fortuneteller provided the customers with Tarot Card readings on weekend nights, and her apprentices showed up on weekdays. I was drinking with my husband's cousin after dinner at the bar, and a well-built woman approached me. She was a total stranger to me, and she was the fortuneteller. She said, 'I can see everything. You had a stalker, didn't you? He was a husband of your neighbor in your apartment.' I was quite surprised to hear that. She also said, 'You'd better stay in this town. Don't go back to Hokkaido. If you return home, you will end up with a divorce.' It turned out that my husband's cousin hired the fortuneteller to tell me these things, you know. How did she know about them?

"Soon, my life in Niigata Prefecture turned out to be unbearable. I just could not stand what was going on there. I came back to Hokkaido with my kids, but maintaining two households was very expensive. It was also difficult to live without Kimura. I still loved him very much. His toxic relatives really affected our marriage. My children saw their Daddy only once or twice a year. For me, it was the case of 'Out of sight, out of mind.' My love and affection for Kimura started to fade gradually, and we decided to get divorced. I kept the last name so that my children's last name and mine remain the same. My kids still keep in touch with him after so many years.

"I started a new job. My children and I were settled more or less in Hokkaido, and we were a happy family. Things were going very well. About six years ago, I fell in love with this good-looking young man who was 15 years younger than I was. He said he was half Ainu and half *Wajin*, just like me. He had very attractive facial features such as thick masculine eyebrows, large round eyes, lush eyelashes, long nose… He was very handsome. He was learning woodcarving in town. It was his occupational training. He was a newcomer and lived in my neighborhood. We soon became boyfriend and girlfriend. I really enjoyed spending time with him, you know what I mean? He was really good!

"By the way, I had a friend who also lived in my neighborhood. She was also half Ainu and half *Wajin* and was my boyfriend's age. She did not drive, so, I used to give her rides to shopping and to other places. I also invited her to supper at my house. I was very good and supportive of her.

"One day, my boyfriend says that he needs to talk with me. I did not think too much about it, and a few days passed. Then, I found his car parked right next to my girlfriend's house, and they were having an affair! I was very upset that my boyfriend was cheating on me, and his partner turned out to be my friend. I was shocked but thought I was not going to have a fight with them. I was really hurt, felt miserable, and shed so many tears.

"It has been some time since I last dated. I am single again, but I am happy having just friends and going out to drink. I do not need a special man, whether an Ainu or *Wajin*. I will never want to marry again."

Lily and I kept in touch via e-mail, and I occasionally called her from my parents' house when I was in Japan. She was always happy to get a call from me. We got together each time I visited her hometown in 2012, 2014, and 2018. Sometimes she brought her daughter or her aunt, who was a few years older than I was. We went for a drive along the Pacific Coast, visited museums, did some shopping in a shopping mall, and ate lunch and dinner a few times together.

I stayed with my Ainu and *Wajin* host families and at an inn during my fieldwork in 2011, 2012 and 2014. Lily would occasionally stop by at my inn after work. An Ainu couple own the inn, and I came to know Sayuri, the co-owner, through Hideki in 2012. In June, Hideki and I had gone to a local festival in town. We had been cooking and eating very delicious Biratori beef and fresh vegetables on a charcoal brazier at our table when Sayuri's father stopped by to say hello. He was Hideki's acquaintance, and he introduced me to him. It seemed to me that Hideki knew all the Ainu people in town. I told Sayuri's father that I was staying at her inn. He must have been glad to hear that, and he kindly had free dessert sent to our table later. In 2014, he agreed to my interviews and appeared in my documentary film.

Sayuri and her husband always keep their inn clean, neat, and very comfortable. They are very friendly and helpful to their guests. Sayuri loves to talk, and I always enjoy staying at their inn with modern amenities.

Figure 91 Inside the inn owned by an Ainu couple. My room is to the right (2012).

Figure 92 The inn's modern toilet with a heated toilet seat, a device with a warm water shower nozzle, and a blow dryer in the commode. There is a sink for washing hands on top of the water tank to conserve water.

Lily and I sit on a cushion on the tatami matted floor in my room facing each other across the low table. We are to have some tea and talk. Sayuri always provides us with a pot of hot water, various kinds of tea, and sweets, which is a custom at the inns and hotels in Japan. Lily and Sayuri are acquaintances, and Sayuri greets us, joins our conversation for a short while, and then leaves.

"I really enjoy talking with you, Kin-chan," Lily says leaning forward.

Lily calls me by my nickname when we are alone but uses more formal Kinko-sensei (*sensei* is a Japanese term used for addressing a teacher, professor, master, attorney, and politician) in public. She wants to appear to be more polite and show respect to me while in public.

"Me, too, Lily! I really appreciate your time and effort that go toward my research," I respond.

"I feel like I can comfortably tell you everything," Lily says.

"I am very glad," I say with a smile.

"You know, everyone knows everyone else's business in this small town, and some people love to gossip," she says.

"Just tell me when you want me to keep things secret or off the record. Once my fieldwork is over, I will be in another country. My mouth is sealed," I say to her with a gesture of closing a zipper on my lips. I wanted to convince her that she could trust me.

"I know you are not a radio station," Lily says laughing.

"Have some more tea and the sweets," I pour hot green tea from the teapot when I notice that there is only a small amount of tea left in her teacup.

"Thank you," Lily says. "You are not eating the sweets?" she asks me.

"No, I need to be on a diet. Sayuri and her husband cook great meals here, and I always eat too much," I tell Lily the reason.

Figure 93 A Japanese dinner at my inn – rice, shrimp fry, salad, tofu with ginger and scallions, pumpkin, nabe (hot pot) with meat and vegetables, and pickles (2014).

Figure 94 A typical Japanese breakfast at my inn - rice, miso soup, eggs, salad, a sausage, pickles, etc. (2014).

"There is so much delicious food in Hokkaido, and I envy you," I tell Lily.

"Plenty of fresh seafood, potatoes, dairy… We are lucky," Lily says.

"I love to eat, but I always need to watch my weight for health reasons. I monitor my weight by writing down the number in my planner every day, and I eat lots of fruits for my breakfast," I say.

"What kinds of fruits do you eat?" Lily asks me.

"I always eat a bowl of blueberries, a banana, an orange, and sometimes I add an apple, a mango, or whatever is in season," I tell her.

"That's a lot of fruit!" Lily says.

"Yes, indeed. But when I am here I really enjoy Sayuri's Japanese style breakfast, too" I tell her.

"Do all Americans eat fruit for breakfast?" Lily asks me.

"I think so, but not as much as I do. I am on a special fruit diet," I respond.

"They normally eat cereals with milk, don't they? At least that is what I imagine," Lily says.

"Many do. In the South, people eat grits, too. Many Americans generally eat eggs, bacon, sausages, pancakes, toast, waffles, and so on. It depends on people's preferences," I say. I am happy to share my life in America with curious Lily.

Lily and I talked about love and romance, work, family, hobbies, and other topics. "I enjoy living here, but I also love to hear more about other places and talk about different topics. You are fun to talk with, and I get a lot of stimulus," Lily complimented me. It also seemed that talking with me helped her become more aware of her ethnicity, tradition, and history. She seemed to be very comfortable being openly Ainu, and she was very happy that I was interested in the Ainu people. I told her that it is very important that the Ainu tradition pass down to the next generation not just for them but also as part of the world heritage. Lily told me during my brief visit in May 2018 that she was inspired by what I said to her in 2014, and she had started to learn how to weave the ancient Ainu textiles that utilize tree fibers. Her teacher is a certified master of the Ainu craft in her 80s. Lily took me to her studio and showed me the colorful yarns with natural dyes. Her master kindly showed me the intricate weaving process. Lily said she wanted to learn the craft as much and as soon as possible.

Toward the end of each of my stays, Lily always asked me, "How many more days do you have in town?" and suggested certain interesting activities such as visiting museums in different cities and towns and talking to the Ainu crafts men and women friends of hers. They were very nice and friendly to me. I enjoyed learning more about their specific crafts such as woodcarving and textile making. I purchased their woodcarvings and good-luck charms that contained the roots of *ikema* to protect people from evil as gifts to my parents, relatives, and friends back in my hometown. I explained to them about my souvenirs, and they appreciated my sharing the information about the Ainu culture, which they did not know at all.

Figure 95 Lily took me to the former residence and clinic of Dr. Neil Gordon Munro (1863-1942). He was a British doctor, archaeologist, and anthropologist. He treated his patients and studied the Ainu people in Biratori before he returned to Scotland.

Lily took me to a local market where they sold vegetables and fruit one afternoon. I purchased some fruit for my breakfast at my Ainu host family for the next two mornings. I also purchased them for her family. We left the store and went to the parking lot. I gave Lily the fruit I just bought. She looked very happy but was very apologetic. She said, "You don't need to do this while you are traveling. I know it costs a lot of money to travel." I said, "Oh, don't worry. I got some financial support for my travel from my parents. Also, these are for your family." Lily looked very happy and said, "Thank you" with a smile.

On a day when we drove long distances to certain towns, I always gave Lily gas money. She would reluctantly accept it. "You know, you are the nicest woman I know. We are friends, and friends do things for free," she would insist. "You have been working for me as an assistant all day, so, please accept the money," I would persuade her. I always try my best to practice "give-and-take" in my relations with others, and so does Lily. We believe in the saying that states, "One good turn deserves another." She stopped by at Mr. Kawanano's residence where I was staying, the day before my departure in 2012.

"Your friend Lily is here! Come down," Mr. Kawanano said when I was packing my suitcase in my room upstairs.

I went downstairs to find Lily standing in the entrance hall. Mr. Kawanano invited her in, but she said she had errands to do and could not stay too long.

"I just wanted to give this to you," Lily said and gave me a small box. "My grandma had a souvenir shop in those days when many tourists flocked to Nibutani. She closed it some time ago, but I found this in a box. I hope you like it," she added. I opened the gift box and found a very nice coin purse with beautiful Ainu designs.

"Wow! It is very nice. I like it," I said to Lily.

"I thought you could use it since you travel a lot," Lily said.

"Thank you so much," I said.

"I'm glad you like it. When are you coming back?" Lily asked me with a smile.

"I will be back next year or the year after. Someone gave me an idea to make a documentary film of the Ainu, and I will try to come up with the money first, and then I will come back," I said.

"Promise me," Lily said.

"Promise," I said.

I took the coin purse and the box that came with it back to the United States. It is too beautiful to use for everyday use, and I still keep it as my treasure and have not used it yet.

Lily is truly a very kind and warm woman. I really appreciate Lily's friendship and liking me as a person, not just a researcher who is interested in the Ainu. Lily once said, "I really am happy that we have become very good friends. As I looked at you taking notes of just about everything Ainu, whether in a museum or during an interview, I started to think that I should record certain things in my notebook for you, too."

When a researcher occasionally misses her informant after her research is finished, it is no longer a pure researcher-interviewee relationship but a real friendship. I know that I will keep in touch with Lily the rest of my life.

Figure 96 Lily gave me this coin purse with very nice Ainu designs, in 2012.

Figure 97 Soba noodles and tempura combination lunch - one of Lily's most favorite Japanese dishes. You pour cold dipping sauce from the porcelain container (top left) to the red bowl (bottom left) and add thinly sliced green onions and *wasabi* (green Japanese horseradish). You dip the cold soba noodles into the bowl and eat. The Japanese eat cold soba noodles mainly in spring and summer.

Figure 98 A warm soba dish that Lily loves. The broth is made with kombu (kelp) and bonito (fish), and the tempura shrimp and vegetables are served over soba noodles along with sliced green onions. We had to wait in line for about an hour to eat this at one of Lily's most favorite restaurants.

Chapter 11: Tomoyo Fujiwara – a Young Working Mother

Figure 99 Tomoyo Fujiwara is a working mother. She felt ambivalent about her Ainu identity when she was younger.

Tomoyo Fujiwara is 30 years old and a mother of two small children. I first met her through a mutual friend of ours in 2012. She lives in a rural area in southwestern Hokkaido. Tomoyo is a working mother, and, unlike her ancestors who had to endure many hardships due to exploitation and oppression by the Japanese government, her life has been very comfortable. I interviewed Tomoyo in 2012 and 2014, and asked her about her life, especially her identity, sense of self, and her family. As with all ethnographic research, this insight into her life and history paints both a rich portrait of the larger human experience and a significant map of a unique and rare culture.[175]

In response to racism, exploitation, and existential inequality, Ainu communities have promoted *exogamy*, the practice of marrying outside of one's racial/cultural group, especially to alter the experiences of future children. Exogamy and other practices explain why, in 1967, Hilger observed that "now the Ainu, who stood apart for millenniums, face complete absorption by the Japanese."[176] The Ainu population was estimated at 13,118 in 2017,[177] but the actual number "remains a mystery."[178] The number reported by the Hokkaido Ainu Association reflects only those who classify themselves as Ainu and are willing to cooperate with the surveyors.[179] There are mixed-race Ainu people who have Japanese ancestors, or ancestors who are members of other groups. In addition, of course, many Ainu prefer not to reveal their heritage due to racism, discrimination, and prejudice, especially when they can pass as *Wajin*.[180]

---

[175] This part originally appeared in Kinko Ito, 2018b.

[176] Mary Inez Hilger. 1967, p.268.

[177] www.pref.hokkaido.lg.jp/ks/ass/H29_ainu_living_conditions_survey.pdf. Accessed 3/5/19.

[178] Barbara Aoki Poisson. 2002, p.5.

[179] Hideaki Uemura. 2008.

Tomoyo Fujiwara was born in 1985 in a district of a small town in Hokkaido where the Ainu population is larger than that of the *Wajin* and where many are of mixed origins. The word *Wajin* generally is used in everyday conversations only in Hokkaido and among the Ainu communities in metropolitan cities in Hokkaido, Tokyo, and its vicinities. I was surprised to hear the word *Wajin* very often in their conversations among both the Ainu and *Wajin* in the town. The *koseki,* or Japanese family registration system, is comparable to the practice of issuing birth certificates in the United States: one must fill in the baby's name, the birth order, and the names of the father and mother. However, the Japanese *koseki* does not require one's race. Whoever was born to a Japanese parent is Japanese. All Ainu people are Japanese, but in communities where both the Ainu and non-Ainu reside, they use *Wajin* to refer to non-Ainu ethnic majority Japanese. In Tomoyo's community, it seems that the Ainu/*Wajin* dichotomy is very prominent in regards to their notion of identity and social status, as well as social types.[181]

Tomoyo's parents had known each other since childhood, but her father was several years older than her mother was. They did not play or go to school together. A mutual friend introduced them when her father was out of school and working, and her mother was in senior high school. They fell in love, got married, and had three daughters. Tomoyo's father was born in 1963, and her grandfather on her father's side is a full-blooded Ainu. Tomoyo said, "My grandmother is half Japanese and half Ainu. My grandfather on my mother's side was half Ainu and half *Wajin* and my grandmother was *Wajin*." According to Tomoyo, her father is "three quarters Ainu" while her mother is "one quarter." She said these numbers with a smile as she tried to think about her family tree.

Tomoyo attended a local elementary school, a junior high school, and senior high school. Upon graduation from senior high school, she went to Sapporo, the capital city of Hokkaido. She went to a beauty school to earn a beautician's license issued by the government. She was encouraged by her parents to leave their small town to study in the big city on her own. Tomoyo said, "I think my parents consider it a social education to get out of the cozy home and live on your own in Sapporo." Her parents also urged one of her sisters to leave town to get some occupational training like Tomoyo. She now has two occupational licenses: barber and kindergarten teacher. Tomoyo said, "You can't obtain beautician or kindergarten teacher's licenses in my home town. My parents only have girls, and I think they encouraged us to get national licenses, which would help us find jobs after having children, or in case we get married but get divorced later. There might be other reasons, but I think these are the primary reasons why they wanted us to get licenses."

In a few years, Tomoyo graduated from the beauty school, became a beautician, and worked in a beauty salon in Sapporo. She said, "When I was working in the salon, it was tough sometimes, and I wished I could quit so many times. However, there were many happy times as well. I would like to work in a beauty salon again if I have a chance. I used to see Takeshi in those days, but since I had to work on Sundays, it was a problem when to see him."

Tomoyo worked in the salon for two years before she got married to Takeshi, a *Wajin* who is also from her hometown. They went back home to live. She explained how she met Takeshi: "My husband and I are very distant relatives, even though there is no blood connection. My father's cousin married Takeshi's aunt. I only knew of my husband's name when I was in elementary school. We went to different elementary schools but the same junior high school. He was very good at baseball, and I belonged to a volleyball club. We used to go to school together

---

180 Hokkaido Shimbunsha. 2018.

181 Yoshihiko Sekiguchi. 2007. Georg Simmel. 1971.

or hang around with our friends talking in the neighborhood parks and playing games. Takeshi and I went to the same senior high school, but he soon dropped out and transferred to a senior high school in Sapporo. In our sophomore year, we 'dated' a little bit. Actually, there are not many places for dating in my town. When he was home from school, I used to go to his house. Since he was in Sapporo, we could only get in touch via cell phone and texting, and when he came back home, we saw each other."

Figure 100 Biratori town does not have many entertainment facilities for the young, but it abounds in beautiful nature for walking and hiking.

When Takeshi and Tomoyo wanted to get married, they did not have any problems. However, Takeshi's family had opposed the marriage of one of his relatives to an Ainu man before. Tomoyo said, "When my husband's aunt, that is, his father's younger sister, wanted to marry an Ainu man, there were a lot of family disputes. The disputes were just terrible, and his family did not like that. I suppose Takeshi's grandparents did not like Ainu people. I wonder if they did not like Takeshi's aunt's husband regardless of his being Ainu or not, I don't know. Luckily, even though I am an Ainu, his family did not oppose our marriage. Maybe it is because we dated for a long time, and I don't think Takeshi's father does not dislike the Ainu. I know a man who is one year younger than I am, a son of a very influential Ainu. We went to the same high school and he dated a *Wajin* girl, but the girl's parents were opposed to their dating saying, 'No Ainu boys!' I think that if a person does not like the Ainu, he would not like his child or grandchild to marry an Ainu. Or, perhaps you do not dislike the Ainu, but when you see their current situation, you might oppose the marriage. With Ainu blood, there might be occasions in which your child or grandchild might be hurt or have a very difficult time. I know a *Wajin* woman in her 60s who told me that just because she married an Ainu, her children and grandchildren sometimes have a hard time. She felt very sorry for them. I think her daughter suffered from discrimination because her father was an Ainu.

"My father says that there are Ainu people who are very talented in a particular field and can do a great job. However, some of them cannot last long in the work place. They quit the job too soon. Some Ainu might be a bit rough and violent, or say or do nasty, inappropriate things to the *Wajin*. Their behavior might have contributed to the negative feelings some people have for all Ainu people. An Ainu individual might work very hard. He might also be very diligent, patient, and non-violent. However, when there are Ainu people who fit the negative stereotypes very well, the individual Ainu who does not fit it also suffers."

When Tomoyo said, "My husband is *Wajin*," with a big smile, she almost looked relieved, very happy, and even proud that she found a nice *Wajin* man. I asked her what kind of identity she has and she said, "I have thought of myself as an Ainu since my childhood. My parents do not hide that they are Ainu. My father is the head of the local branch of the Hokkaido Ainu Association, and my mother loves Ainu dances and embroidery. They always tell me and my sisters to be proud of our heritage."

Tomoyo's family speaks only Japanese as in many other Ainu homes today, but their conversation is peppered with Ainu words. Her father often uses Ainu words such as *pirika menoko* (beautiful woman), *wakka* (water), *tuki-pasuy* (a spatula-like Ainu tool for transmitting one's wish to God), and *kamuynomi* (prayer for God). Tomoyo said,

"My family uses some Ainu words jokingly in our conversation, but to me, the Ainu language is an ancient language that people do not use in the modern era. The Ainu words are from the past. When I hear certain Ainu words I understand the meanings, but I do not use them often except when my mother, my sisters, and myself use them just for fun. Someone says 'Can you pass me those *pasuy*?' and I know he or she is talking about chopsticks. *Tuki-pasuy* is an Ainu's ceremonial spatula, but today *pasuy* only refers to chopsticks. The other one might say, '*Iyayraykere*' (Thank You) in return when they are passed. Once there was a stray dog near our house, and my father said, 'Whose *seta* is it?' When our father uses Ainu words, we sisters sometimes may look at one another and say, 'Why is he using an Ainu word?'"

Regarding her identity, Tomoyo said that she is ambivalent about being an Ainu. She said:

"I am very happy I am an Ainu, but at the same time I feel ashamed… I don't understand the system very well, but when I was in senior high school, I got a scholarship. When I went to the beauty school in Sapporo, I went to the Department of Ainu Policies and registered myself. I got money from the Hokkaido Ainu Association, and my parents also helped me financially for two years while I was in Sapporo. When your parents belong to the Ainu Association, you automatically are entitled to a scholarship.

"I had attended the Ainu Language School in town since first grade and went abroad because of this connection. I went to the language classes offered by a *Wajin* professor once a week for about two hours. I really enjoyed the class sometimes, but at other times, I thought I would rather not go, like when I had difficulty memorizing certain Ainu words, which I felt was a nuisance. I like the sound of the voices of the old men and women talking in Ainu in a certain manner. However, they seem to speak with special mannerisms, using unique voices and idioms, and I do not understand them. I just love the sound though. I went to the language school from the first grade to the 9th grade, but I cannot remember all the words now. I can still sing Ainu songs for dancing or say tongue twisters. We did not have textbooks at the school. Our teacher gave us handouts each week, and we studied them.

"Not all children living in my community went to the language school. Their parents wanted to hide their Ainu identity. They have not 'come out,' and if the kid didn't know that he or she was an Ainu, the parents wanted to keep it that way. It is seldom the case that a person in this community would voluntarily say 'I am Ainu.' Even when others are talking about the Ainu, I wouldn't say 'I am Ainu,' either. I am proud of being an Ainu, but I have mixed feelings about making my Ainu identity public. There are many Ainu people living in the community, and there is not much prejudice toward the Ainu here. However, there are people who have prejudice. For example, there are *Wajin* students who might say, 'You are an Ainu, aren't you?' as a joke to another *Wajin*. If they say the same to an Ainu, it is considered as bullying. There are situations in which I can comfortably say 'I am an Ainu' though.

"Sometimes the *Wajin* say things that insult the Ainu. They are kids, and they may not really know who the Ainu are, but they make condescending comments. I have never been exposed to that, but I think it was during my puberty, when I was in junior high school, that I felt ashamed of being an Ainu. Like, I am very hairy. 'Why was I born an Ainu?' I would ask my parents, and they would say 'You are cute because you are an Ainu'."

I asked her how she deals with her hairiness when I felt that Tomoyo was comfortable talking about matters that are more private. She said, "I shave my arms. You can bleach the hair, but that makes it glittery and stands out against your skin color. As for my face, I shave my face including my eyebrows, which tend to become a uni-brow. I love my thick eyelashes, but I do not like my body hair too much. My body hair grows really fast, and I have to shave once every three days or so. My sister has two strands of hair on her big toes, you know, just like those Japanese men who have hair at the bottom of the big toes. I do not have that hair and I boast about it to my sister," Tomoyo laughed.

Tomoyo became more aware of her Ainu identity when she went abroad for the first time in an elementary school. She said, "When I was in the 6th grade, I had an opportunity to visit Canada for 10 days with the teachers and junior high school students from the Ainu Language School. There were only 15 children between the fourth and the 8th grade. I think there were five elementary school children. There were several adult leaders and translators. We drove to Sapporo, and flew to Narita (Tokyo International Airport) and then to Vancouver, which was extremely beautiful. From Vancouver, we flew in a very small propeller airplane to a place where there were many small islands. We did a homestay there for a few days and did cultural exchange. I stayed in a home that included the oldest man on the island. I played with the children in the neighborhood, and we rode boats. We went to a school on our last day and visited with the indigenous people. I was really impressed with their dynamic and energetic dances, and then we performed our Ainu dances. I think it was the very best performance we had ever done. Until then I did not have any feelings about whether I was happy as an Ainu or not. To tell you the truth, I had felt a bit shy about being an Ainu and was even embarrassed with our dances until I went to Canada. Those young people said to me, 'I am a native Canadian who belongs to such and such indigenous tribe' with so much pride that I thought that they were really cool. I thought, 'I need to have pride as an Ainu as well.' They taught me that it was not an embarrassing thing to be an indigenous person. It was a rather cool, wonderful thing to be proud of."

Tomoyo also became more self-consciousness when she became a teenager. She said, "When I was in puberty, I started to dislike myself as an Ainu because of my hairiness. Our town holds an Ainu cultural festival in the town auditorium every year, and our Ainu language school would present traditional dancing and singing, and perform a play. I was worried that my classmates from my junior high school might notice me perform Ainu dances or participate in the play. The dances and play give the Ainu their identity, and they brand the performers as Ainu. I also didn't want my classmates to know that I was going to the Ainu language school. I did not want to perform in the cultural festival. My teacher would not insist that I should perform. She said, 'If you don't want to join us, it is okay.' I hardly participated in the cultural festival when I was in junior high school.

"I had not experienced prejudice, insult, or bullying myself, yet I did not want to be labeled as an Ainu. In those days, there were people who looked down on the Ainu as a whole. Once they labeled me as an Ainu, they would put me into that category. I could become a target of prejudice, discrimination, and bullying.

"I really have mixed feelings about the Ainu. I need to do something for the Ainu, but I can do this only when I make it public that I am an Ainu. I can't do that because of my worries about how people see me. I don't want my children to have these same worries about this identity problem. I had an Ainu friend, a boy whom I was interested in when I was in the 10th grade. My parents warned me that if I wanted to marry this Ainu boy, my children would have problems. My parents know his parents, too. They have a pride in their heritage, but they did not want me, or my sisters, to marry an Ainu. This sent me a mixed message and gave me mixed feelings about being an Ainu. If you marry an Ainu, your children might not like being Ainu, but they have to live with it for the rest of their lives. You cannot get away from your blood."

Tomoyo's experiences as an Ainu are quite different from those of her distant ancestors, and they also differ from her grandparents' experiences in a more contemporary Japan. For instance, Ainu men in their 80s in her town told me that their lives were harsh when they were younger. For example, the men experienced persistent prejudice, discrimination, and bullying at school and at work in those days. One elderly man told me, "When we kids had a fight, my *Wajin* teacher used to scold and blame me all the time just because I am an Ainu." Another said, "I quit junior high school due to [my bad experience with] this female *Wajin* teacher." Yet another explained, "There were 47 students in my class, and four of us were Ainu. The Ainu were not considered human beings. Yet there were 50 to 60 young Ainu men from town who went to war and died for Japan." The *Wajin* women who married Ainu men also told me about their problems with both their in-laws and with people in the communities where they lived.

At school, Tomoyo enjoyed hanging around with her friends, and she had not experienced any bullying. This is partly due to anti-bullying efforts on the part of the teachers and the PTA. It also had something to do with the small student population in the 1990s. Tomoyo had only six classmates in the same grade at her elementary school. Her junior high school had students from three different elementary schools in town, which exposed her to more *Wajin* students. In puberty, she became more conscious about her heritage. However, Tomoyo is beautiful, attractive, and can pass as *Wajin* easily, which could be one of the reasons why she did not feel so alienated.

Additionally, Tomoyo benefitted from recent social policy initiatives that were unavailable to older Ainu, which certainly explains some of the disparity in perspective. Government programs to assist those of Ainu ancestry include low-interest (2%) mortgages, scholarships for high school and university students, infrastructure programs aimed at improving roads and sewage disposal facilities in communities where Ainu live, salaries to those who teach Ainu crafts, and more.[182] Yet Tomoyo also benefited from living in a rural community where the Ainu outnumbered non-Ainu Japanese. The community was characterized by *Gemeinschaft*-like associations. The people share the same ancestry, common values, norms, and mores; everybody knows everybody. However, the ascribed status in her town entails the entrenched dichotomy of Ainu vs. *Wajin* that can be traced to the 1700s and earlier.

"Who is an Ainu? Is it blood or culture that makes one an Ainu?" I asked Tomoyo. "I think both," she reasoned. Sekiguchi, who studied the Ainu in the Tokyo metropolitan area, states "their existence as human beings cannot be framed by a single identity" because the boundaries between the Ainu and *Wajin* could be ambiguous.[183] Due to the systematic and constant promotion of exogamy, the racial boundaries are indistinct, as Tomoyo showed in her struggles to identify race in her ancestry. Sekiguchi's interviewee Mr. H moved to Tokyo when

---

[182] Ito, Kinko. 2014a.

[183] Sekiguchi, Yoshihiko. 2007, p.238.

he was in the fifth grade. Sekiguchi states, "Mr. H identifies as an Ainu because of his blood. He does not know the 'culture'; but because of his 'blood' he considers himself an Ainu."[184] He continues, "Let's suppose that the mixed blood is a common occurrence among the Ainu: then the categories of Ainu vs. *Wajin* do not have lucid boundaries, and his identity is ambiguously situated."[185]

Tomoyo's self-conception fluctuates between being an Ainu and being a non-Ainu Japanese. Sometimes she feels more of an Ainu, and she is proud of her Ainu heritage due to her socialization at home, while at other times she does not think about her Ainu identity. Her sense of self changes in different social settings, among different groups of people, and it depends on how she defines herself. According to Hamaguchi, a Japanese social psychologist, one's notion of the self is *kanjin*, or "a situated self" that exists among the whole (e.g., groups of individuals) and is dependent on the context of one's social relationships. Hamaguchi calls *kanjin* "the contextual," a subject who always behaves in relation to other subjects in the shared and mutual life space. One's self is found and confirmed only within one's relationship to others. Hamaguchi argues that this phenomenon is shown more commonly and strongly in Japanese than in other nationalities. Japan's social attributes stress interdependence, mutual trust and reliance, and human relationships (as opposed to egocentricity, self-reliance), and human relations as a "means" rather than as an "end."[186]

We can explain the Ainu vs. *Wajin* dynamics best by using Georg Simmel's notion of *social types*. Just like "the stranger," "the mediator," and "the adventurer," the Ainu is a particular social type that is characterized by attributes of the social structure and interactive relations. In other words, the Ainu are given assigned positions and expected to play certain roles. Social types are viewed through the lens of what is done to them by society.[187] Tomoyo benefited from scholarships given to the Ainu students, attended the Ainu language school, and went to Canada to do cultural exchange with the native people near Vancouver. Certain numbers of Ainu are poor and on social welfare. However, the majority of the Ainu are independent and engaged in tourism, selling Ainu crafts and performing Ainu dances and singing as well as other occupations.[188]

When she was a teenager, there were certain tender moments when Tomoyo felt ashamed of being an Ainu. Her junior high school had more *Wajin* than Ainu students. In puberty, her hairiness reminded her of her ancestry, and she did not like it. She went to the Ainu language school but did not want her new classmates to know it, nor did she want to appear in Ainu cultural festivals. For her, performing Ainu dances and Ainu plays equaled Ainu identity, and put one in a particular social category. What Tomoyo thought other non-Ainu Japanese classmates thought of her participating in Ainu performances influenced how she felt about herself as an Ainu. This is an excellent example of *the looking-glass self*: Tomoyo imagined the ways her classmates perceive her performing the Ainu dances, she imagined how they would evaluate her and label her an Ainu, which would peg her in a certain social category and social situations, and she felt bad and withdrew from the activities.[189] However, in her elementary school days, her

---

[184] Sekiguchi, Yoshihiko. 2007, pp.145-146.
[185] Ibid.
[186] Hamaguchi, Eshun. 1996.
[187] Simmel, Georg. 1950.
[188] Kayano, Shigeru. 2009.
[189] Cooley, Charles Horton. 1964.

experience with the native people of Canada and the Ainu dances she performed there made her feel proud of being an Ainu.

Tomoyo's mixed feelings about being an Ainu might come from her socialization, especially from her interactions with her parents who told their daughters to be proud of being Ainu, but warned them against marrying an Ainu. As Tomoyo said, "You cannot get away from your blood." Having an Ainu parent ascribes one Ainu status, yet in one's *koseki* paper (the Japanese family registration system); there is no mention of one's race. Because most contemporary Ainu are of mixed origins, being an Ainu seems to depend solely on one's personal definition.

Being an Ainu always made Tomoyo feel ambivalent about her identity, particularly during puberty. She loves the Ainu, but she does not like certain Ainu. She is proud to be an Ainu, but she felt embarrassed about belonging to a subculture. She loves Ainu dancing, but she did not want to perform Ainu dances in front of her non-Ainu classmates at a cultural festival.

Tomoyo told me that she loves Ainu culture and wants to embrace it fully. She said: "When I am dancing an Ainu dance, I feel very excited and happy. When I am watching an Ainu dance, even when I do not join it, my body starts to move to the music by itself. When my children are bigger, I would like to join the adult section of the Ainu language school and learn traditional Ainu ballads. I want to embroider traditional Ainu embroidery, make kimonos -- there are so many things I want to do."

As for her small children, Tomoyo wants them to experience the Ainu culture firsthand. She always tries to bring them to cultural events held in her hometown. At the age of 30, she feels happy about being an Ainu and wants to do something for the preservation of the culture in the future. When I was leaving town, she said, "I am very happy you are studying the Ainu. I really appreciate your interest." Tomoyo and I are Facebook friends and we occasionally exchange e-mails, too.

Chapter 12: The Story of Mr. Fukuji Kaizawa: An Instructor of Woodcarving

The first time I saw Mr. Fukuji Kaizawa was on the morning of May 30, 2012. He was walking near his store while I was riding with Hideki, a staff member from a museum whom I befriended during my first visit in 2011. He kindly offered me help when I told him via e-mail that I wanted to visit and interview the Ainu people in 2012. Hideki obtained permission from his boss to give me a ride from the airport and help me with my interview schedules. He also gave me rides along with his friends and co-workers so that I could get around easily.

"That old man over there looks very different. He actually seems exotic," I said pointing at the man walking in a short distance.

"*Ahh*, he is an Ainu man who owns this souvenir shop right here," Hideki said and stopped his car. I could see many of his folk art merchandises displayed in his shop from Hideki's car.

"I see. Do you think I can interview him? Do you think he would mind?" I asked.

"No. I'm sure he will be happy. Go visit his store when you have time today," Hideki said.

"Okay, I will," I told him.

I walked to Mr. Kaizawa's store from the museum in the afternoon.

Figure 101 Mr. Fukuji Kaizawa wearing traditional Ainu clothes and a head crown for religious rituals in his store.

I open the door and enter the store saying "Hello!"

"May I help you?" Mr. Kaizawa stops his hands and looks at me. He thinks I am a customer.

"Yes. My name is Kinko Ito, and I came from America. I am very interested in studying the Ainu," I introduce myself handing him my business card.

"*Ahh*," he says.

"May I interview you?" I politely ask him. *I really hope he says yes*, I am a bit anxious.

"Sure! Please sit down on this chair. We can talk," he says and smiles.

I feel relieved since he looks happy to have me in his shop. Thus, our interview begins.

Mr. Kaizawa calls his souvenir shop Fuku-chan Mingeiten, or Fuku-chan's Folk Art Shop. He sells his hand-made crafts, mostly woodcarving. He gives me his business card that says "Woodcarving Direct Sales Shop." His title is instructor of woodcarving.

"So, the name of your store comes from your nickname, Fuku-chan?" I ask him.

"Yes," he says. "You can call me Fuku-chan, too."

The Japanese suffix *chan* is usually used for nicknames for girls and young boys. It is also used for men and women of any age among friends. It is a term of endearment, familiarity, and fondness. Now I call him Fuku-chan, and it seems to bring us closer together. Even though it is our first meeting, I feel like he is my friend and feel more comfortable. I end up spending three hours with him drinking tea and sweets. Fuku-chan generously shared with me his experiences in his youth and adulthood.

Fuku-chan was born in the Nibutani section of Biratori in November 1936. Nibutani is one of the few communities in town where the majority of the residents are of Ainu origin. His mother was born in Niikappu. His parents moved to Nibutani after a tsunami hit the region. "The tsunami came over from Tomikawa, and it damaged the Niikappu area. That is why my parents decided to come here and live on a higher ground," he says. Fuku-chan was born as the fifth and the last child. He had a brother and three sisters. His elder brother, who was the first son, was 11 years senior to Fuku-chan, and unfortunately, his sisters died young. His uncle and aunt went to Manchuria, and his uncle died there. His aunt came back to Japan after WWII, but she died of tuberculosis. Fuku-chan's parents took care of their three children.

"My brother went to war when I was in the first grade. He later was retained in Russia. I still remember the day he left. We lined up along the road to the horse ranch, waved Japanese flags, and sent him off to war," Fuku-chan comments.

"What was it like to live during the war?" I ask him.

"There was a food shortage, and to make matters worse, poor harvests lasted for about three years. Food was rationed, and we had a very difficult time. Luckily, we Ainu have great survival skills in nature. We had various preserved foods such as *heneimo* potatoes, dried mountain vegetables, and preserved fish. *Wajin* people often depended on the Ainu people to exchange things with food," he says.

"What are *heneimo* potatoes?" I ask Fuku-chan.

"We freeze the potatoes during the cold winter. We soak them in water, peel the skins, and mill them. We put the potato powder in a mortar, add boiling water, and make dumplings. You make patties and fry them on a frying pan. The Ainu in those days put in sardine oil and ate them, but today we use butter or sugar. *Peneimo* potato patties were Ainu's preserved food, and they stayed in your stomach for a long time," he explains.

"I see. Do you speak Ainu?" I ask him.

"No, I don't. My parents did not speak the Ainu language due to the assimilation policy and the bullying many Ainu children experienced at school. Speaking Ainu was prohibited by the government, and my parents followed the rule to a fault and spoke only Japanese. I once went to a folk art craft fair with my works, and someone spoke to me in Ainu. I did not understand the words but wrote them down on a piece of paper. I asked my mother what they meant. I became interested in Ainu language then," Fuku-chan replies.

Fuku-chan has several traditional Ainu garments, a sword, a head crown, and other items on the walls of his shop. I knew an Ainu word for the head crown. I wanted to show off my knowledge of the language just like the day at the *Poroto Kotan* when they did a quiz show.

"That is a s*amanpe*, right?" I say with lots of confidence pointing at the head crown hanging on one of the walls. He bursts into laughter, saying "A beautiful girl like you should not say that word!"

I do not understand what he means.

"What did I say?" I ask him.

"You should have said *sapanpe*," he explains.

Sapanpe is a head crown worn by Ainu men for rituals and formal occasions as well as when they want to welcome guests from far away.

The word I used, *samanpe*, is very similar to *sapanpe*. There is only a letter difference, that is, "m" and "p." However, the meanings are very different.

"*Samanpe* means women's here," Fuku-chan touches his crotch in a similar manner like Michael Jackson used to do on stage.

"Wow!" He looks so funny, yet I get a bit embarrassed that I called the religious head crown "a female sex organ" in Ainu. I was so proud and wanted to show off my knowledge of the word, but ended up saying something totally inappropriate!!

"I am sorry I said the word, but it's so funny!!" I apologize and laugh.

"It's okay," Fuku-chan is forgiving.

This incident really breaks the ice between us, and Fuku-chan seems to be really enjoying talking with what he calls "a beautiful girl from America" who is more than 20 years junior to him.

Figure 102 One of Fuku-chan's woodcarvings that I purchased at his store. At the bottom is a *korpokkur* (a dwarf from Ainu folklore)[190], and a *kotankorkamuy* sits on the leaf of a butterbur plant that the short man is holding. *Kotankorkamuy* literally means "a god that owns a village" and refers to a Blackiston's Fish Owl. It is an animal god of the Ainu people.[191]

"When did you start woodcarving?" I ask him.

"I went to Mr. Kikujiro Kaizawa's house when I was four or five years old. I was very interested in his work. I was given a knife and made a snake when I was eight years old. I could teach wood carving to adults when I was in the 6th grade," Fuku-chan says.

"It sounds like you were born to be a woodcarver," I say.

"I became a certified professional wood carver, and he also taught traditional Ainu wood carving techniques. Wood hates moisture, and the dryness is the key. Wood is very delicate. I have been carving for more than 60 years now," he proudly says. "My father was also very good at working with wood, and he also helped build Nibutani Elementary School," he adds.

"Did you teach woodcarving full time?" I ask him.

---

[190] Tsunoda Yoichi. 2018, p.62.

[191] Tsunoda Yoichi. 2018, p.84.

"No, I did other jobs, too. For example, Kadowaki Group in Mukawa asked me to work for them as a carpenter near Lake Shikotsu for six years. It was before the Sapporo Winter Olympic Games, which was in 1972. I did woodcarving in the winter time," he says.

"Did you like being an instructor? What was it like?" I ask him.

"When I started working as an instructor, my students called me *An-chan*, or Bro (elder brother)," he says.

"That's very informal," I say.

"They treated me as if I was a kid (since I was young). I was determined to be called by more respectful Kaizawa-san or Kaizawa-sensei within a week, and I worked very hard," he says.

"What kind of teacher were you?" I ask.

"When I was working with other Ainu men, I told them that they should do their best, especially when they were looked down upon by the *Wajin*. I said 'We are Ainu, but hard work and persistence always pays off.' I know an Ainu man who worked for a factory, where he was always called 'Ainu, Ainu' and mistreated. He had a breakdown and became neurotic. I personally am happy being born an Ainu, but even now, some *Wajin* people look at me and say 'Ah, inu!'[192] I am called 'a dog!' It happens in a city like Tomakomai, you know," he says.

"I am sorry about that," I tell him.

"My mother always urged me to study hard at school. The Ainu people were often cheated by the cunning *Wajin* who wanted to take advantage of uneducated Ainu. However, I quit junior high school because of my homeroom teacher. She was a *Wajin* and was very nasty to me. I was discriminated against just because I was an Ainu. I suffered from acute pneumonia and did not go to school for three months. I was cured by penicillin, which was worth several months of my father's wages. When I returned to school, I was forced to sit next to a very bright student so that I could get help catch up. In those days, Koreans and the Ainu were looked down upon by the *Wajin*. It was much worse than today. We were categorized as 'Chosun and Ainu.' There were men from Korea who married Ainu women after WWII, and they remained in Japan for a while. They decided to go to Korea to live. I know a couple whose child died on the ship. I heard that the child was buried at sea," Fuku-chan comments sadly.

"How did you meet your wife?" I try to ask him to lighten up the mood.

"You know, I was not very popular with women. I met my wife at work. She was working for a store where I sold my folk art items and woodcarvings," he comments. Currently Fuku-chan lives with his wife in their house, and he has his own workshop in his store in the center of Nibutani.

An old woman visits Fuku-chan's shop.

"Hello!" she says as she opens the door and enters the shop.

"Oh, hello! How are you?" Fuku-chan says.

"I'm fine. I just stopped by to say hello," she says.

"*Konnichiwa!* (Hello!)" I say to her bowing. I am much younger than she is, and I need to show due respect to her age.

"*Ahhh, konnichiwa!*" she says and bows to me lightly.

"Is she your customer?" she asks about me to Fuku-chan.

"No, she is a professor from America and is interviewing me for her research," he says happily.

"Oh, you are helping her with her research. What is it about?" she asks.

---

[192] The word Ainu can be phonetically split into "ah" and "inu (dog)."

"I am studying the Ainu," I respond.

"Okay. I will not stay too long and bother you. I just wanted to check on you, Fuku-chan. So long" she says.

"Thank you for stopping by! So long!" he sees her off.

"Is she an Ainu?" I ask Fuku-chan.

"No, she is a *Wajin* and we have known each other for a long time," he says.

"How can one tell that a person is an Ainu?" I ask him.

"The Ainu are hairy. When a certain Ainu man I knew took a bath with *Wajin* in a public bath, he was very surprised how hairy he was as compared with *Wajin*. He wanted to shave off his body hair saying, 'Why am I so hairy?' I think he was ashamed of his hairiness. I am an Ainu but am not hairy. I used to wish I had more hair on my chest actually," Fuku-chan says.

"Does it make you more masculine?" I ask him.

"I think so. By the way, there are also hairy people in Okinawa. Did you know?" he asks.

"I heard about it. Hokkaido and Okinawa are somehow connected when it comes to some racial characteristics. I read it somewhere that they both keep the DNA of ancient Japanese when Japan was connected to the continent and the Japan Sea was a lake," I comment.

"That's why we call them *Okinawa Ainu*," Fuku-chan says.

"I see," I say.

"My Ainu friends who visited Okinawa told me that they met their 'brothers' there. Hokkaido and Okinawa are so far away, but the bros shared the same facial features," he commented.

"You said you are happy you were born an Ainu. Can you give me examples?" I ask him.

"There was a lack of food here during WWII. Poor harvest occurred for about three consecutive years. Food was rationed, and many people experienced food insecurity everywhere in Japan. We Ainu luckily had knowledge of survival in the wild. We had various kinds of preserved food. We utilized *heneimo* (preserved potatoes), harvested *kitopiro* (*gyōja ninniku* in Japanese: ascetic garlic), and dried mountain vegetables. We also boiled the meat of deer and bears and made smoked meats. We also preserved salmon. The Ainu tried to hunt bears while they were hibernating, but the meat does not taste as good right after being hunted and slaughtered," he says.

"So, the food was still abundant in nature," I comment.

"I used to enjoy going to the river to catch big fish. We would go to *hori*, a place where fish lay eggs, use a devise called *marek*. It is a revolving harpoon, or hook. People also set a weir fish trap to catch fish coming up the river. We would cook and invite our neighbors and eat together in the middle of the night," Fuku-chan says.

"In the middle of the night!? Why?" I asked.

"Because it was prohibited by the Japanese government to catch salmon in the rivers. Salmon was called *kamuycep* (God's fish), and there were so many of them in those days. I love *ruybe*. It is salmon caught in winter. It is left outside after their innards are cleaned. It freezes in the cold temperature. We sliced the fish and ate the meat like *sashimi*,[193]" Fuku-chan comments.

"The salmon which was caught at the beginning of the season was placed on a wooden chopping board and dedicated to the God of Food. We would pray 'Please let salmon come up the river in abundance so that everyone can eat it. Wild salmon tastes the best, and those farm-raised salmon are smaller and not as tasty," he adds.

---

[193] Sashimi is sliced raw fish eaten with wasabi horseradish and dipped in say sauce.

"I am glad you had food during the war. Many Japanese starved to death due to the lack of food," I comment.

"The Japanese government prohibited catching salmon in the rivers and hunting deer. But the Ainu are generous people, and we always help and support others. There are no homeless people among the Ainu. When we betray our own kind, we get ostracized," he says.

Figure 103 A side view of Fuku-chan wearing a sapanpe.

Figure 104 Fuku-chan and the author dressed in traditional Ainu attire in his shop.

"Wow! I'm sorry I have taken so much of your time," I apologize to Fuku-chan when I realize that a few hours have passed by.

"It's okay," he says.

Fuku-chan had only me and the old woman coming to his shop during the afternoon on that day. I heard from an Ainu woman during my visit in the previous year that Biratori used to be one of the most popular and busy sightseeing places several decades ago, but it has not been attracting many tourists due to a new highway that bypasses the town to other cities that attract more tourists. "It used to be a lot busier here before the new highway was constructed," Fuku-chan said.

I took notes of what Fuku-chan said and several photos of him. He was all smiles. Later Fuku-chan said I could try on the Ainu clothes (a kimono and a headband) for women that were hung on one of the walls of his store. He got excited and smiled when I told him I was more than

happy and honored to try them on. He helped me get dressed, and we took several selfies together. He seemed to be really enjoying the time with me. He showed me a traditional dance that the Ainu perform when they go to war and when they win a victory. I asked him if I could videotape him with my digital camera since his performance was full of energy and power.
Six months passed after my interview with Fuku-chan. One day in November 2012, I received an e-mail from Hideki.

"I am very sorry to tell you, but Fuku-chan passed away yesterday. He was 76 years old."

I was at a loss to hear the news that came all too soon. I called Hideki to get more information about what had happened since Fuku-chan looked in very good heath when I visited him in June. Hideki said that he had certain health issues just like any other elder. Very good friends of mine had passed away in November 2009 and 2010, and I was very sad about another loss in November. At the same time, I felt lucky and good that I had taken photos of Fuku-chan and me and a very short video of Fuku-chan performing an Ainu victory dance. I really wished that I had taken more photos and video clips.

Fuku-chan's death was an awakening for me as a researcher. I realized that it is indeed very important to record the elders' stories and hear their perspectives on their lives RIGHT NOW. Moreover, I needed to record them as a primary source. They speak about their lives in their own words instead of in my written words, which make their stories secondary sources. Thanks to another summer scholarship I received from the Dean's office, I went back to Biratori in 2014 to shoot video clips of these Ainu elders' talks.

Chapter 13: The Story of Kayoko – a *Wajin* woman who married an Ainu

I met Kayoko through Hideki in 2011. She was a *Wajin* woman in her mid-60s and was married to an Ainu man who used to be a farmer. He was much older than Kayoko, and he was in a nursing home when I visited her. She, Lily, and Hideki had worked together on certain Ainu-related township projects before, and they were friends in spite of the age differences. Kayoko is a very friendly and nice woman. Hideki, Kazuya (Hideki's friend and Kayoko's acquaintance) and I were invited to stay overnight at her house when I visited Biratori in 2012.

"Let's have a party! We have plenty of room in our house, and I can accommodate all of you. If you stay overnight, you do not have to worry about driving drunk on your way home. You can drink to your hearts' content with me!" she said when Hideki and I happened to see her in town.

"I will be expecting you guys about 4 p.m.," she said.

"We need to visit some places before we come, but we will make sure to be there about that time," Hideki said.

"Okay, see you then! Oh, don't forget to call Kazuya!" Kayoko said.

"OK! See you!" Hideki said.

"See you!" I said, and we parted with her.

The day of Kayoko's party came soon enough. Hideki had to do some errands, but we arrived at Kayoko's house shortly before 4 p.m.

"Welcome! You are always on time!" Kayoko says to Hideki, smiling at the entrance.

"Thank you for your invitation. Kazuya just called me and said that he is finishing his job and will leave as soon as possible," Hideki says.

"I just called Lily if she is available, and she said she can join us for a few hours," says Kayoko.

"Lily's coming, too!?" I ask her excitedly. Lily and I met in the previous year, and we became good friends.

"The more, the merrier! Come in! Come in!" Kayoko invites Hideki and me cheerfully.

"You can use one of the rooms next to the kitchen, and there are two rooms upstairs to sleep in," Kayoko says. "Pick any room you want."

"Maybe Kazuya and I should sleep upstairs, and Dr. Kinko can stay downstairs," Hideki says. He is giving me more space, which is a sign of respect, or maybe he felt more comfortable sleeping on different floors. This arrangement actually worked very well for me since I did not want my male friends to hear my snoring, which occasionally sounds as if a tornado is approaching!

"It doesn't matter whoever gets whatever room. I will be sleeping upstairs in my room," Kayoko says.

"Okay, I will take this room," I say to Hideki and set my luggage there.

"I'm going upstairs to leave my backpack," Hideki says.

Her party starts when Kazuya arrives.

"Hi, Kazuya! How are you doing lately?" Hideki asks him.

"So-so, you know. It's the same job over and over again," he says.

"Hi!" I greet Kazuya. He seems to be a bit shy.

"Hi!" he says, and Hideki introduces me to him.

"You three stay in the living room, and please start drinking," Kayoko says.

"I brought some beer for you," Hideki says and opens a big brown paper bag.

"Thank you. Just put it on the table there," Kayoko says.

"Okay," Hideki replies.

"I am sure Lily will be here in no time," Kayoko says looking at the clock on the wall of the living room. She leaves and begins heating dinner in the kitchen. I can hear her chopping something at the sink.

"Kayoko-san, do you need any help?" I say peeking out of the door. I notice that she has finished several dishes already.

"No, I will be just fine. You can just relax in the living room!" she says. In many households of Japan, the hosts expect their houseguests to do nothing but drink liquor and use chopsticks. Some women are still adamant that no guest enters her kitchen or helps her prepare food.

"Hello!" Lily opens the entrance door, takes her shoes off, dons a pair of slippers for guests, and enters the living room. Obviously, Lily has been to this house before. She knows where the party is.

"Hi, Lily!" The three of us welcome her.

Kayoko sets the table in the dining room and gathers us as if we were her children saying "Dinner time! Come over!" She looks very happy and content. She first offers us *sake* and beer with *otsumami*, a Japanese finger food that accompanies drinking. I do not drink, and Kayoko gives me cold Chinese Oolong tea, which looks exactly like whisky, especially on the rocks. This way everyone seems to be drinking alcohol, a courtesy to make a non-drinker blend in with the drinking bunch. Actually, their proverb says, "A nail that sticks up gets hammered down."

"Oh, I have non-alcohol beer, too, if you prefer," Kayoko says.

"No, thank you. Oolong tea is just fine," I say.

It is a Japanese custom not to pour your own drink at the table, so I keep pouring alcohol for the rest of the members.

"I am obliged, thank you so much," Hideki says. He seems to love drinking.

"I can pour my own drink. You don't have to be bothered, okay?" Lily says.

"Me, too," Kazuya says.

"Okay, you pour your own drink then," I tell Hideki.

"No, when a beautiful woman like you pours alcohol, it always tastes better," he says jokingly.

"You are talking about bar hostesses, right?" I ask him.

"Everyone should be responsible for his or her own drinks, okay?" Kayoko says.

"Thank you, Kayoko-san. That way I can enjoy tasting your home-cooked meal better," I say.

Kayoko says, "Feel free to help yourselves to all these dishes. There are more in the kitchen if you want seconds, or even thirds. All the vegetables come from my farm and the mountains nearby."

"And you went to the nearby river to catch the fish for *sashimi*[194]?" I say laughing.

Kayoko laughs and says, "No, I special-ordered these fresh *sashimi* from a fish shop in the next town, especially for you guys!" I appreciate her hospitality very much.

---

[194] *Sashimi* refers to sliced fresh fish (e.g., tuna, white tuna, yellow tail, red snapper, calamari, octopus, etc.) and is eaten with green *wasabi* horseradish and dipped in soy sauce.

Figure 105 Fresh and delicious sashimi.

Figure 106 Various seasonal mountain vegetables Kayoko harvested and cooked.

Figure 107 A bamboo shoot dish in season.

When Kayoko asked me what I liked to eat a few days earlier, I told her that I really like a leafy vegetable called *gyōja ninniku* in Japanese. Its name in Ainu is *pukusa* or *kitopiro*. The word *ninniku* means garlic, and it thus has a very strong smell. The Ainu boil or stir-fry this vegetable, and use it as a seasoning for soup and meat dishes, too. It has medicinal properties and cures common colds, bruises, and skin diseases. Its particularly stinky smell makes it a perfect protection charm from evils.[195]

Figure 108 The sign says *gyōja ninniku* 120 yen (about US$1.10) per bunch.

I first ate *gyōja ninniku* at Mr. Kawanano's house in 2011. Motoko, his wife, cooked it for dinner, but she was not sure whether I would eat it due to its very strong smell. I fell in love with its bold taste instantly! Believe it, or not, my fatigue from traveling disappeared quickly, and I felt happy and extremely energetic the next day. *Gyōja ninniku* definitely has some health benefits just like regular garlic.

Figure 109 *Pukusa* (gyōja ninniku) with eggs.

[195] Yoichi Tsunoda. 2018, p.120.

Figure 110 Homemade fresh salad. Biratori is well known for its tomatoes, which are grown in green houses.

On the dining table is a plastic bottle of pills.

"What are these pills for?" I ask Kayoko.

"Take a few pills, and your breath will not stink. This way you can eat the dish as much as you like without worrying about offending others!" she replies.

Figure 111 Pills that get rid of bad breath.

All of us kept drinking, eating, and talking until late that night. Kayoko said. "I prepared a hot bath for you. You can bathe and then go to bed. Okay?"

"Well, I must be going. Thank you for the invite. I really had a great time," Lily says and leaves the house. We say good night to her.

"I am going to bed right now. You guys can pick any of the extra bedrooms, and behave yourselves!" Kayoko says.

"Kayoko-san, I am a married man, you know. Of course, I will behave myself. But I am not sure about the rest!" Hideki says and laughs.

"No, no! I am a very good boy, so I will behave myself," Kazuya retorts.

"I think I am going to sleep, too. Good night, Kayoko-san! Thank you so much for everything," I say and go to my room with the view of the garden on the first floor.

Hideki and Kazuya go upstairs to a room adjacent to Kayoko's bedroom.

"Kayoko-san!!" I hear Hideki knocking on her door and calling her name.

I can hear lots of commotion going on for some time. *They must be having a pillow fight or something*, I think. The three of them, the drunkards, are laughing and talking as if they were junior high school students on a school trip.

Figure 112 Just about all the ingredients for Kayoko's home-cooked meal came from her garden. She enjoys growing vegetables, and she gets up early and stays up late at night to tend her garden in the summer time.

I had a chance to interview Kayoko on another day, and the following is what she told me about her life in Hokkaido. Here is her story.

Kayoko was born to her *Wajin* parents in 1948 in the part of the Kuril Islands which became Russian territory in 1951. Her father worked as a mechanic, and her parents had three daughters. Kayoko's two elder sisters were born in Hokkaido. When Kayoko was one year old, the family came back to Hokkaido. Her parents then got divorced. Her father had custody of her and her siblings, and he remarried when Kayoko was four years old.

"I was brought up by my father and step-mother. They had a son and a daughter together, and I still get along very well with my stepsiblings. I did not know anything about my birth mother. When I was 35 years old, my birth mother and I were reunited after she spent years searching for me. For our first meeting, we met in a very nice hotel in Sapporo. My sisters did not want to meet her since they thought that she 'abandoned' them. My mother came to my town two years after that initial meeting and stayed for two months. She returned to Sapporo. Then, six years later, she came back to me, and I took care of her until her death."

Kayoko has been married to an Ainu man for the last 40 plus years. She readily admits that her marriage has been rather rocky, and she still is bitter about it. She thinks it really was a mistake.

"How did you meet your husband?" I asked Kayoko.

"I worked at a confectionary company in Sapporo when I was young. I used to belong to a club supported by the company and played sports. There was an Ainu man from this town who had business with the company, and he suggested for me to have an arranged meeting with my future husband. He wanted to be a matchmaker. It was at the beginning of the 1970s, and the gravel roads were being turned into paved roads with asphalt," she said.

"I met my future husband at a sushi restaurant with the Ainu go-between. He later threatened me saying, 'You should marry this Ainu man, or else I will lose face.' 'I would force you to work at a hostess bar if you don't marry him,' the go-between added. Actually, he said he would 'sell' me into that kind of sleazy business" Kayoko said.

I did not understand why this Ainu man wanted to be Kayoko's matchmaker. What are the reasons for forcing her to marry his friend? I suspected some kind of previous dealing between Kayoko and him, but I refrained from asking her the reason for his actions. It sounded bad enough, and I was afraid that she might be offended if I really wanted to know too much about her personal matters.

Kayoko continued, "I married the Ainu man and had a son and a daughter. Before our 15th wedding anniversary, my husband suffered from a cerebral hemorrhage and became blind and disabled. I had been taking care of him at home for a very long time. When his condition worsened, I sent him to a nursing home. I still go there and check on him occasionally.

"My husband was a drinker and was very abusive. The other day when I visited him at the nursing home, he was drinking alcohol secretly. He used to say to me as he grabbed my chest, 'I am going to kill you!' I don't know why he did it, but he did it for no reason. He blamed all his problems on me. He would hit me and threaten me since the beginning of our marriage. When I didn't respond to his accusation, he would say 'Why are you ignoring me? What the hell are you thinking about!?' Once I was cooking in my kitchen chopping with a knife, and he started that kind of bullshit again. I got so furious with him that I threw the knife at him. It flew by my daughter, who was in the second grade at that time. Luckily, it missed her and stuck in the wooden TV stand," Kayoko said.

"I regret marrying him. I am a friendly person and want to get along with people who are around me. I want to help those who are in need. That is how I generally feel about people. However, I just cannot get along with my Ainu in-laws. They have way too many problems such as debts, bad incidents at jobs such as tardiness and disrespectfulness, conflicts with their relatives, etc. In addition, there is the reality that they have been discriminated against just because they were born Ainu.

"I have been lucky because I always had a job. I think my in-laws are jealous of me, and that is part of the reason why they act the way they do toward me. Nepotism is rampant in rural areas. It is not who you are, but who you know, and with whom you are connected and associated that determines whether you are hired or not. Your qualification, knowledge, and skills sometimes do not matter at all. Once a person becomes a public servant, he or she remains in the job until retirement. The person cannot be fired even though there are problems. Some are incompetent, have no manners, suffer from mental illness, or cannot get along with others well. If you snitch on such a person, there are consequences. You may become a victim of ostracism, bullying, and discrimination, just to name a few."

This kind of phenomenon has something to do with what sociologists call gatekeeping. Gatekeepers determine who to admit to the positions of power, status, and wealth in society. When a gatekeeper is of one race, the other races often encounter a very difficult situation attaining the positions. Kayoko had advantages in society just because she is a *Wajin* while her Ainu in-laws are not. This may be the reason why they seem bitter to her without reason. Institutional racism and gatekeeping have systematically oppressed the Ainu, who tended to have fewer educational and employment opportunities than the *Wajin*. They generally tend to face more discrimination in dating and marriage as well.

Kayoko said, "In this rural area everyone knows everyone else. Everyone has a certain position assigned to him or her, and he or she needs to act accordingly. I am *Wajin*, and my husband is Ainu. I am a city girl, and my husband grew up in a rural town. We are different. My husband has four brothers, and they cannot get along well with one another, either. They all seem to hate me. They have bad attitudes toward me for some reason, and it has been going on for decades now. Some in-laws do not like me and have not spoken to me for more than ten years now.

"I got married and moved to the community. My health was not good, and I was rather weak. I previously had five miscarriages before my daughter was born. A seventh child was stillborn. We went to the hospital in a bigger city in an ambulance, but the baby died right after he was born.

"My husband had a cerebral hemorrhage at 50 years of age, and he became disabled. I had to become the breadwinner to support my family. It was great to have a job outside of the house since I did not have to spend time with my husband all the time. We have this huge tract of land here, and I love to farm. However, when I hire men to work on my farm, my in-laws suspect that I am having an affair with them. They always think the worst of me," Kayoko said.

I sympathized with her and asked her why she got married to her abusive husband in the first place. Didn't she know better than to remain in the bad marriage?

Kayoko said, "It's a long story. When I was in Sapporo, I fell in love with this *Wajin* man. We had been almost engaged when my boyfriend found something wrong with his lung. My father and stepmother were totally against the marriage because of his health, and my boyfriend sort of evaporated. I did not know his whereabouts at all.

"I missed him so much. I took 100 sleeping pills and drank alcohol while taking the pills. Luckily, my sister found me and took me to an emergency room in an ambulance. I was lucky I did not die. After this incident, I quit my job and left for a sanatorium. The following two years were nothing but hell. I did not want to live, and I was mentally unstable. I was a wreck. It was then when the arranged meeting with the Ainu man took place in this town. The go-between said, 'Unless you say yes to this marriage, I will not let you go back to Sapporo.'

"When I was preparing goods and furniture necessary to start a new life before my wedding, my old boyfriend appeared all of sudden at my apartment in Sapporo. He said that his lung would heal very soon, but he did not know what was going on with my life. I was about to marry an Ainu man whom I did not love at all. My boyfriend and I cried and cried, and I was amazed by the quantity of tears that we shed together. Eventually we parted."

I then asked Kayoko why she did not get divorced from her abusive husband. She said, "I did not want to get divorced for the sake of my children. We sent them to a high school and then college. My daughter got married and has two children now."

Her husband's domestic violence continued even after he had the cerebral hemorrhage. Kayoko said, "When he gets violent, his face changes its shape and color. His face becomes pale, his skin has goose bumps all over, and he gets excited. Up until five years ago or so, I was so terrified that I never retorted or retaliated. Lately, I declared to him that I would not do anything that I do not want to. His body has been weakening, and he now has Alzheimer's disease as well. He still begs others to give him money, runs up his debts, and drinks even though he is in a nursing home. I just cannot let him do all these things and cause problems for me and my children. You know, the Ainu have a tradition of sharing. However, I see disparity between their great tradition and their behaviors such as hatred and jealousy. I married an Ainu, and I became a member of their family, and they hate me."

In spite of all the problems and troubles that Kayoko faced throughout her married life, she is now spending a more peaceful life at home. Her husband is in a nursing home, and she is no longer a victim of his abuse. She enjoys working with her co-workers at her job. Kayoko feels very happy surrounded by the love of her son and daughter and two grandchildren. Kayoko said, "This is the best time of my life. I enjoy working in the yard growing vegetables and flowers. I am happy now."

I am glad that Kayoko is content and made peace with her life regarding her marriage even though her Ainu husband abused her and their children. It seems to me that domestic violence was common among certain Ainu families in those days.

An elderly Ainu woman told me about her family. She said, "My father worked as a farm laborer and as a material selector of lumber in the mountains. My mother was from Akita and was a beautiful woman. She used to say to me, 'You are ugly but good enough to look at.' She delivered telegraphs to the houses in the mountains and grew vegetables in summer. We lived with my grandmother until I was six years old. She spoke Ainu even though I spoke only Japanese.

"My father was an ordinary man, but he used all the money he earned on drinking. He thought he was entitled to use it as he liked. He would drink *shōchū* elsewhere and beat up my mother when he returned home to find a visitor. I think he was jealous because my mother was a beauty. He spent all his earnings on liquor, which made our family very poor. I could not go see a movie since I was in the third or fourth grade. I could not leave my poor mother behind because my father would get drunk and beat her.

"As for me, he loved me because I was the only child. My mother had to work hard and she purchased an insurance plan for 1 yen a long time ago. I received a call telling me that I could get the money from an office in Tokyo in 1977. I received 83,000 yen! I was very thankful to my mother and cried with joy. I wished that he had been here. I could have taken her on trips, you know.

"Many Ainu men had drinking problems that led to their financial problems. They would purchase liquor on credit and when the liquor store found that they could not pay with cash, they demanded to pay by land. My grandfather was a very smart man. The Ainu language does not have letters, but he could write Japanese beautifully. However, he was a hardcore drinker. He would drink and drink. He divorced his wife and gave her custody of their children. He became an old man and came to live with my family. He did not cause us any trouble because of his age.

"My mother passed away in 1944 and my father in 1945. A typhoid epidemic occurred in Mukawa at the end of August. Someone from our village went to a funeral and brought back the disease. His funeral lasted for three days. Twenty people, who were mostly old and weak, died of typhoid in September.

"I visited my uncle's house in 1951. He asked me to go purchase *shōchū* for *kamuynomi* (prayers). My uncle introduced me to an Ainu man, his acquaintance, and I got married. We did not have a wedding ceremony. I have been married for 60 years, but my life has been difficult. Now I teach Ainu language classes supported by many people. This is the happiest time of my life. "

About the Author

Kinko Ito is a professor of sociology in the Department of Sociology and Anthropology at the University of Arkansas at Little Rock, U.S.A. She received her Bachelor's degree in British and American Studies from Nanzan University in Nagoya, Japan and her Master's and Ph.D. degrees in Sociology from the Ohio State University. Her Ph.D. dissertation title is "Organizational Adaptation of Japanese Companies in the United States."

Professor Ito has written numerous articles on *manga* (Japanese comics) in academic journals such as *International Journal of Comic Art*, *Journal of Popular Culture*, and *Japan Studies Review*. Her other articles appeared in *Asian Popular Culture*, *Japanese Visual Culture*, *Mangatopia,* and *Grōbaru Kyōiku* (Global Education). She published *A Sociology of Japanese Ladies' Comics: Images of Life, Loves, and Sexual Fantasies of Adult Japanese Women* (Edwin Mellen Press) in 2011.

Her ethnographic research on the Ainu people started during her sabbatical in spring semester 2011. She visited the Ainu people in Hokkaido in 2011, 2012, and 2014 and interviewed both the Ainu and *Wajin* (non-Ainu ethnic majority Japanese) people. She also took photos and shot video clips of their everyday life and artifacts. Sociologists have traditionally depended on verbal and written data for their research. Only in the last several decades have they started to utilize visual information such as advertisements, photographs, documentary images, and videos for their analysis.[196] With this new dimension of sociology in mind, Dr. Ito has used multimedia to present her ethnographic data and analysis of the elderly Ainu's lives in contemporary Japan. She produced her first documentary film in 2015 and her second one in 2018. *Have You Heard about the Ainu? Elders of Japan's Indigenous People Speak* (78 minutes) and *Have You Heard about the Ainu? Part 2 Toward a Better Understanding and World Peace* (31 minutes) are available on YouTube. She also visited Biratori Town again in 2018 and invited her main informants who later became her friends to a luncheon.

With her pen name K.I. Peeler, Dr. Ito has published several Kindle books about her world travels and other topics for the general audience: *My Fiji! A Short Trip to Paradise for Less Than US$1,000, Hello Colombia! A Short Trip to Bogotá and Medillín, Kidnapped!? In Istanbul and Other Stories from Turkey, Pantyless in Scandinavia and Other Escapades of World Travel, Gourmet Food, Scrub, and Happiness in Body and Seoul: A Short Visit to South Figure 18Korea, Tetas de Deseñador y Meditación Zen: Comó Suvreviví al Cáncer de Seno y Sigo Feliz en América* (in Spanish), *Designer Boobs and Zen: How I Survived Breast Cancer and Stay Happy in America*, ああ　フィジー　4泊5日10万円オバサン2人の珍道中, and 愛する人を亡くしたら (in Japanese). These Kindle books are available at Amazon.com and other Amazon sites of the world for US$3.99 each.

---

[196] Timothy J. Curry and Alfred C. Clarke, 1978. Erving Goffman, 1979.

Figure 113 Professor Kinko Ito is dressed in a *cikarkarpe*[197], a traditional Ainu kimono (2011). The dress has Ainu design cotton appliques with embroidery. She is also wearing an embroidered *matampus* (headband). The handwoven bag is called *saranip* in the Ainu language. The clothes and the bag belong to Mrs. Motoko Kawanano in Biratori Town.

[197] *Cikarkarpe* is also called *Kaparamip*. Tsunoda, Yoichi. 2018, p.149.

Bibliography

Ainu Minzoku Hakubutsukan. (eds.) 2009. *Ainu Bunka no Kiso Chishiki* (Basic Knowledge of the Ainu Culture). Urayasu, Chiba: Sofukan.

Ainu Minzoku ni kansuru Jinkenkyōiku no Kai (eds.). 2017. *Irankarapte Ainu Minzoku wo Shitteimasuka: Senjūken, Bunkakeishō, Sabetsu no Mondai* (Hello – Do You Know the Ainu? The Problems with Indigenous Rights, Cultural Transmission, and Discrimination). Tokyo: Akashi Shoten.

www.ainu-assn.or.jp. Accessed 4/10/17.

www.//ja.wikipedia.org/wiki/アイヌ語.

www.ainu-museum.or.jp/en/info/midokoro.html.. Accessed 3/9/17.

Asahi Shimbun 10/30/11. "Ainu Minzoku no Seijidantai Kesseie…Saninsen Yoritsu Mezasu." (Toward the Formation of the Ainu Political Organization to Send a Politician to the House of Councilors)

Batchelor, Rev. John. 1892. *The Ainu of Japan: The Religion, Superstitions, and General History of the Hairy Aborigines of Japan.* London: The Religious Tract Society. (2011. Reprints from the collection of the University of Toronto Libraries. Lexington, KY.)

Benedict, Ruth. 1986 (orig.1946). *The Chrysanthemum and the Sword.* Tokyo: Charles E. Tuttle Company.

Biratori Town Homepage. www.town.biratori.hokkaido.jp. Accessed 5/5/19.

Christopher, Robert. 1983. *The Japanese Mind.* New York: Fawcett Columbine.

The Chunichi Shimbun. 2014. *Nihon no Senjūminzoku Ainu* (Ainu: The Indigenous People of Japan). Sunday Edition. 1/12/14.

Conley, Dalton. 2017 (5th ed.). *You May Ask Yourself An Introduction to Thinking Like a Sociologist.* New York: W. W. Norton.

Cooley, Charles Horton. 1964. *Human Nature and the Social Order*. New York: Schocken.

Cultural Survival Quarterly, June 2001.

www.culturalsurvival.org/publications/cultural-survival-quarterly/japans-ainu-seek-help-preserve-their-native-culture. Accessed 9/3/18.

Curry, Timothy J. and Alfred C. Clarke. 1977. *Introducing Visual Sociology*. Dubuque, Iowa: KENDALL/HUNT PUBLISHING COMPNAY.

Feagin, Joe R. and Clairece Booher Feagin. 1996. *Racial and Ethnic Relations*. Upper Saddle River, N.J.: Prentice Hall.

FRPAC (The Foundation for Research and Promotion of Ainu Culture). 2010. *Together with the Ainu: History and Culture*. Sapporo: FRPAC.

FRPAC (The Foundation for Research and Promotion of Ainu Culture). 2012. *Ainupuri—Ainunokokorowotsunagu*. Sapporo: FRPAC.

FRPAC (The Foundation for Research and Promotion of Ainu Culture). 2001. *Ainu Seikatsubunka Saigen Manuaru: Tabemono - akikara fuyue-* (The Manual for Reconstruction of Ainu Life and Culture: Food – from autumn to winter). Sapporo: FRPAC.

Fujimoto, Hideo. 2006. *Gin no Shizuku Furufuru Mawari ni – Chiri Yukie no Shōgai*. Tokyo: Sofukan.

Fumoto, Shinichi. 2008. *Kindai Nihon to Ainu Shakai* (Modern Japan and the Ainu Society). Tokyo: Yamakawa Shuppansha.

Hall, Edward. 1977. *Beyond Culture*. Garden City, NY: Anchor Press/Doubleday.

Hamaguchi, Eshun. 1996. *Nihongata Shinrai Shakai no Fukken*. Tokyo: Toyo Keizai Shimposha.

Henshall, Kenneth G. 2004. *A History of Japan: From Stone Age to Superpower*. 2nd ed. London: Palgrave Macmillan.

Hilger, Mary Inez. 1967. "Japan's 'Sky People,' the Vanishing Ainu." *National Geographic*.131: 2:268-296.

Hilger, Mary Inez. 1971. *Together With The Ainu: A Vanishing People*. Norman, OK: University of Oklahoma Press.

Hokkaido Ainu Association. www.ainu-assn.or.jp. Accessed July 23, 2012.

www.pref.hokkaido.lg.jp/ks/ass/H29_ainu_living_conditions_survey.pdf. Accessed March 5, 2019.

Hokkaido Shimbunsha (ed.). 2018. *Kokoro Yurasu Mizukara no Ainu to Deai Ikiteiku*. Sapporo: Hokkaido Shimbunsha.

Ito, Kinko. 2018a. *Have You Heard about the Ainu? Elders of Japan's Indigenous People Speak Part 2 Toward a Better Understanding and World Peace*. YouTube.

Ito, Kinko and Paul A. Crutcher. 2018b. "An Oral History of a Young Ainu Mother: Tomoyo Fujiwara Talks about Her Experiences in Contemporary Japan." *Japan Studies Review.* Vol. 22:137-154.

Ito, Kinko. 2015. *Have You Heard About The Ainu? Elders of Japan's Indigenous People Speak* (a documentary film: 78 min). YouTube.

Ito, Kinko. 2014a. "An Elderly Ainu Man's Story: Ethnography." *Japan Studies Review.* Vol. 18:117-133.

Ito, Kinko. 2005. "A History of Manga in the Context of Japanese Culture and Society." *Journal of Popular Culture 38*(2):456-475.

Ito, Kinko. 2004. "Teaching Japanese Culture and Society: A Pedagogical Strategy for American College Students and an Implication for Global Education." *Gurōbaru Kyōiku*. Tokyo, Japan. 6:2-12.

Ito, Kinko. 2000. "The Manga Culture in Japan." *Japan Studies Review* 4:1-16.

Ito, Kinko. 1998. "Japanese Language (Nihongo)." in *Modern Japan*. (Ed.) James L. Huffman. New York: Garland Publishing. Pp. 106-107.

Ito, Kinko. 1993. "Teaching the Sociology of Japan." *Teaching Sociology* 21(4):371-376.

Kawanano, Kazunobu and Kayano, Shiro. 2011. Personal communication.

Kawanano, Kazunobu. 2012. Personal communication.

Kayano, Shigeru. 2004. *The Ainu: A Story of Japan's Original People.* Boston: Tuttle Publishing.

Kayano, Shigeru. 2009. *Ainu no Ishibumi.* Tokyo: Asahi Shimbun Shuppan.

Kendall, Diana. 2013. *Sociology in Our Times.* 9th ed. Belmont, CA: Wadsworth Cengage Learning.

Kikuchi, Isao. 2002. *Ainu Minzoku to Nihonjin Higashi Ajia no nakano Ezochi* (The Ainu and the Japanese Ezo in the East Asia). Tokyo: Asahi Shombunsha.

Kikuchi, Isao. 2010. *Sugae Masumi ga Mita Ainu Bunka* (The Ainu Culture Masumi Sugae Observed). Tokyo: Ochanomizu Shobō.

Kojima, Kyoko. 2009. *Emishi Ezokara Ainue* (From *Emishi Ezo* to Ainu). Tokyo: Yoshikawa Kōbunkan.

Kono, Motomichi. 2002. *Ainushi Gaisetsu* (Introduction to Ainu History). Sapporo: Hokkaido Shuppan Kikaku Sentā.

lewallen, ann-elise.2016. *The Fabrics of Indigeneity AINU IDENTITY, GENDER, AND SETTLER COLONIALIMS IN JAPAN.* Albuquerque: University of New Mexico Press.

Maconis, John J. 2012. *Sociology.* 14th ed. Boston: Pearson.

Matsuura Takeshirō Kinenkan, brochure. Matsusaka, Japan: Matsuura Takeshirō Kinenkan.

Ministry of Justice. www.moj.go.jp/JINKEN/jinken05_00004.html. Accessed on 12/3/12.

Namikawa, Kenji. 2010. *Ainu Minzoku no Kiseki* (The Trajectory of the Ainu). Tokyo: Yamakawa Shuppansha.

Noda, Satoru. 2018-2019. *GOLDEN KAMUY.* Volume 1 – 17. Tokyo: Shueisha.

Nomura, Giichi *et. al.* 1996. *Nihon no Senjyū Minzoku Ainu* (Ainu: The Indigenous People of Japan). Osaka: Buraku Kaihō Kenkyūjo.

Ogasawara, Nobuyuki. 2004. *Ainu Sabetsu Mondai Dokuhon* (A Reader on Ainu Discrimination). Tokyo: Ryokufū Shuppan.

Ooyama, Shingo. 1992. *Matsuura Takeshirō no Shōgai.* Mikumo-cho, Mie: Mikumo-cho.

Poisson, Barbara Aoki. 2002. *The Ainu of Japan.* Minneapolis: Lerner Publications Company.

www.pref.hokkaido.lg.jp/ks/ass/new_jittai.htm. Retrieved 11/19/15.

Reischauer. Edwin O.1990. *Japan The Story of a Nation.* 4th ed. New York: McGraw-Hill Publishing Company.

Saneimukku, Jikū tabibito bessatsu. 2017. *Imakoso Shiritai Ainu.* Tokyo: San-ei Shobo.

Sato, Sadao and Ooyama Shingo. 1995. *Matsuura Takeshirō – Kōhō Mikumo Keisai Shūyakushū (April 1998 – March 1993).* Mikumo-cho, Mie: Mikumo-cho Yakuba.

Schaefer, Richard. 2000. *Racial and Ethnic Groups.* 8th ed. Upper Saddle River, NJ: Prentice Hall.

Segawa, Takuro. 2007. *Ainu no Rekishi: Umi to Takara no Nomado* (The History of the Ainu). Tokyo: Kodansha.

Segawa, Takuro. 2015. *Ainugaku Nyumon* (Introduction to the Ainu Studies). Tokyo: Kodansha.

Sekiguchi, Yoshihiko. 2007. *Shutoken ni Ikiru Ainu Minzoku* (The Ainu Who Live in Tokyo Metropolitan Areas). Urayasu, Japan: Sofukan Co.

Simmel, Georg. 1950. *The sociology of Georg Simmel.* New York: Macmillan Publishing.

Simmel, Georg. 1971. *On Individuality And Social Forms.* Chicago: The University of Chicago Press (Selected Writings: Edited and with an Introduction by Donald N. Levine).

Therborn, Göran (ed.). 2006. *Inequalities of the World.* London: Verso.

Tsuda, Nobuko. 2000. "Ainu Bunka no Fukugen to Densho o Mezashite – Seikatsuyohin o Fukugensuru Densho no Jissen o Tooshite." *Kita no Seikatsu Bunko Vol. 10. Hokkaido no Seikatsu Bunka.* Sapporo: Hokkaido.

Tsunoda, Yoichi. 2018. *Zukai Ainu* (Schema Ainu).Tokyo: Shinkigensga.

Uemura, Hideaki. 2008. *Ainu Minzoku Ichimon Ittō* (Questions and Answers On the Ainu). Osaka: Kaiho Shuppansha.

Ushiro, Hiroshi. Ph.D. The Historical Museum of Hokkaido. Personal communication. 6/9/12.

www.//ja.wikipedia.org/wiki/ウエペケレ (uepeker). Accessed 4/19/17.
www.en.wikipedia.org/wiki/Louisiana_Purchase_Exposiiton. Accessed on 4/5/17.
Wolferen, Karel van. 1989. *The Enigma of Japanese Power: People and Politics in a Stateless Nation.* New York: Alfred A. Knopf.

Zaidan Hōjin Ainu Bunka Shinkō Kenkyū Suishin Kikō (ed). 2007. *Heisei 18nendo Fukyū Keihatsu Seminā Hōkokushū.* (Reports on the Seminars on Spreading Enlightenment in 2007).

Made in the USA
Monee, IL
03 August 2023

40401664R00088